# About the Author

Chris Bailey ran a year-long productivity project where he conducted intensive research, as well as dozens of productivity experiments on himself, to discover how to become as productive as possible. He has written hundreds of articles on the subject and has garnered coverage in media as diverse as *The New York Times*, *HuffPost*, *New York* magazine, *Harvard Business Review*, TED, *Fast Company* and *Lifehacker*. The author of *Hyperfocus* and *The Productivity Project*, Chris lives in Kingston, Ontario, in Canada.

# How to Calm Your Mind

## Finding Productivity in Anxious Times

## Chris Bailey

MACMILLAN BUSINESS

First published 2022 by Viking, Random House LLC and Random House Canada

First published in the UK 2022 by Macmillan

This paperback edition published 2024 by Macmillan Business
an imprint of Pan Macmillan
The Smithson, 6 Briset Street, London EC1M 5NR
*EU representative:* Macmillan Publishers Ireland Ltd, 1st Floor,
The Liffey Trust Centre, 117–126 Sheriff Street Upper,
Dublin 1, D01 YC43
Associated companies throughout the world
www.panmacmillan.com

ISBN 978-1-0350-0199-6

1 3 5 7 9 8 6 4 2

A CIP catalogue record for this book is available from the British Library.

Printed and bound by CPI Group (UK) Ltd, Croydon, CR0 4YY

Visit **www.panmacmillan.com** to read more about all our books
and to buy them. You will also find features, author interviews and
news of any author events, and you can sign up for e-newsletters
so that you're always first to hear about our new releases.

*For my family*

You are the sky. Everything else—it's just the weather.

Pema Chödrön

# Contents

## Why We Need Calm

did not intend to write this book. A few years ago, I plunged deep into a state of burnout, and soon after experienced an anxiety attack while speaking in front of an audience of one hundred people (a story I'll share in the first chapter). Out of necessity for my own mental health, I dove headfirst into the science surrounding the topic of calm: poring through journal articles, chatting with researchers, and running experiments on myself to try out the ideas I encountered and try to calm my mind.

I write about productivity for a living—and really enjoy doing so. In the midst of my burnout and anxiety, though, my thinking was alternating between restlessness and insecurity. If I was exhausted and anxious while deploying the very productivity strategies I was writing about, what right did I have to give that kind of advice in the first place? Something was missing.

Fortunately, after digging deep into the research, I found a very different idea from the one I had been telling myself. Driven initially by self-preservation, which quickly turned into a curiosity I could not extinguish, I discovered how misunderstood the state of mind we call calm is, to the extent that it is understood at all. While it's true that anxiety—the opposite of calm—is our responsibility to deal with, many of the factors that lead us to feel anxious are *hidden from view*, making them difficult to identify, let alone tame.

I'm probably not the only person who has been feeling more anxious than usual. I type these words in 2022, two years into what we all know has been a particularly stressful time. If anxiety has creeped in for you, too, know you are not alone, and you shouldn't beat yourself up over it. Certain sources of anxiety (and stress) are easy enough to spot, like a global pandemic, news about war, or having an overly demanding job. But many more sources are neither obvious nor apparent—including the ones we'll cover in this book. Some of these factors include the extent to which we're driven to accomplish more; the numerous *invisible* sources of stress buried within our days; the "superstimuli" we tend to regularly; our performance against the six "burnout factors"; our personal "stimulation height"; the amount of time we spend in the digital world compared with the analog one; and even what we eat and drink. These sources of anxiety are the metaphorical dragons I would eventually encounter in my journey to calm.

In this book, I'll break down these ideas and more. Luckily, there are practical, tactical strategies—many of which you can invest in right away—that can help you overcome anxiety and burnout, all while reclaiming calm.

As my experiment to tame stress and burnout while finding calm progressed, I was relieved to discover that the productivity advice I'd been giving wasn't wrong. It was, however, missing a critical piece of the productivity picture.

Productivity advice works. *Good* productivity advice (there's a lot of fluff out there) helps us take control of our time, attention, and energy, which frees up mental and calendar space for what's meaningful. That enriches our lives. It also reduces stress and lets us stay on top of things. Given all we have to juggle, this is more essential today than ever before.

But it's also crucial that we develop our *capacity* for healthy productivity in our lives and work. When we face anxiety and burnout, we become less productive without realizing it.

Investing in calm is the way to maintain and even grow our capacity for productivity.

Finding calm and overcoming anxiety make us more comfortable in our own skin, while at the same time helping us to feel at home inside our mind. We build a larger, more expansive reservoir of energy from which we can draw throughout the day. This allows us to work productively and live a good life. By bringing more calm to our day, we invest in the missing piece that fuels our efforts—in work and life—to become *sustainable over time*. Encountering the ideas in this book, I felt all of the productivity advice I had been giving lock into place with a satisfying *click*.

During this journey to calm, my productivity levels rose dramatically as I became less anxious and burnt out. With a calm, clear mind, I could write and connect ideas with relative ease; when I would typically have written several hundred words, I found myself penning a couple thousand. With less anxiety I became more patient. I listened more deeply and became far more engaged *with whomever I was with and in whatever I was doing*. My thoughts were crisp, my ideas sharp, my actions more deliberate. I became more intentional and less reactive, my mind no longer frazzled by outside events. And I connected with the purpose behind my actions, which made my days feel more meaningful.

In practice, the productivity benefits of calm can be profound. And regardless of your circumstances—including if you have limited time, budget, or energy—calm is attainable. This book explores the strategies that will help get you there. (We'll see just how much time calm earns us back in chapter 8.)

This leads us to an exciting conclusion: even *after* setting aside the plentiful mental health benefits of calm, reducing anxiety is worth our time. Because calm makes us more productive, we more than make back the time we spend trying to achieve it.

As I went through my personal journey, I began capturing all that I learned about the topic of calm into something that vaguely resembled the outline of this book. I started the process reluctantly, knowing I'd need to reveal the more challenging, personal parts of my story. But the phenomena of anxiety and burnout are too universal to *not* talk about. By sharing my journey and the lessons I've taken from it, I hope to clear some of the path to calm for you, too.

We're living through an anxious time. And assuming that you don't live under a rock, there seems to be an awful lot to worry about. I'm not going to rehash those reasons (we hear enough about the world's problems), but it's worth saying that it's tough not to feel anxious in the modern world.

Calm isn't about ignoring reality. Instead, it provides us with the resilience, energy, and stamina to navigate this ever-changing environment. While I initially sought calm as a means to overcome anxiety, I've come to see it as the secret ingredient that has led me to a deep presence with whatever it is I'm doing. And because it makes us more productive, we shouldn't feel guilty for investing in it.

On the surface, calm is the opposite of a sexy productivity hack. Yet, much like the yeast in bread or the dash of salt in your favorite recipe, even *trace* amounts of calm improve our life, helping us to feel present and happy. An even greater amount of calm leads to far more, letting us feel focused and comfortable in everything we do. Calm provides us with roots, making us more engaged and deliberate in our actions. It makes life more enjoyable while *also* saving us time—and what is better than that?

By the end of the book, I hope you'll find the same thing I did: that in an anxious world, achieving calm is the best "life hack" around.

How

to

Calm

Your

Mind

## CHAPTER ONE

## The Opposite of Calm

didn't think of calm as something worth seeking until just a few years ago. Usually when I've felt calm, I've stumbled into the feeling by accident: relaxing on a beach in the Dominican Republic after disconnecting from work; surrounded by loved ones over the holidays; or finding myself with no plans or obligations at the start of a long weekend.

Aside from happy accidents like these, calm has not been something I've sought out, found attractive enough to pursue, or even paid much mind to. That was, until I experienced a total absence of it in my life.

Unfortunately for me, I can pinpoint the exact date (and time!) when it became evident that all traces of calm had fallen out of my days; this realization coming to a head in an instant, like a cast-iron bathtub plummeting through the floor of an old apartment building.

As I mentioned in the preface, I was onstage when it happened.

Anxiety, the opposite of calm, touches everyone differently: for some, it's an ever-present companion; for others, it's a rare occurrence. For me, anxiety has always been a low-rumbling presence. It was on this day in particular that this rumbling anxiety—which had been growing steadily noisier for several years, as the stress of work travel accumulated—erupted into a full-blown panic attack onstage in front of a one-hundred-person audience.

Moments before the talk, waiting to go onstage, I felt . . . off. My mind raced far more than usual. It was as though I could keel over at any moment and give in to what felt like a bout of vertigo.

Luckily for me, I snapped back to attention as my name was called.

Bounding up the stairs and grabbing the slide clicker, I dove right in to my talk. A minute or two in, I was feeling pretty good, and the dizziness had subsided. Then it happened: an all-encompassing, sinking feeling engulfed my entire mind and body as I plummeted into a deep pit of nervousness.

I felt as though someone had injected my brain with a vial full of liquid terror. As I stammered and stumbled on my every word—there might as well have been a dozen marbles in my mouth—beads of sweat began to form on the back of my neck. My heart rate escalated, while I again felt like fainting; my pre-talk vertigo feeling was back for round two.

I pushed ahead, stumbling through my talk on autopilot. Gripping the podium so I wouldn't fall, I apologized to the audience that had gathered there to see me. I blamed my sweating and stammering on having a bad case of the flu, which I think they bought (thankfully). In my mind, this also engendered enough sympathy to get through the rest of my talk, even though I still felt like giving up, walking off the stage, and never looking back. I finished the speech to a lukewarm reception.

I considered that a win.

Immediately following the speech, head down, I took the elevator up to my hotel room, where I collapsed on the queen-sized bed. With a slightly more settled mind, I replayed the events of the day in my head. The whole time was a blur, a series of events so nebulous and stuck together that nothing was distinguishable from anything else. My fists clenched as I did my best to relive my faltering onstage, cringing at the memory.

I also played back the previous night, when I arrived at the hotel.

Stepping into my room after a long day of travel—one day of travel in a string of many others—I took a bath, one of my favorite ways of relaxing on the road (that and a substantial amount of delivery food, obviously). If I have enough time to spare the night before a talk, I'll almost always take a soak in the tub, while listening to nerdy podcasts, relieved to have gotten to my destination on time.

The night before this particular talk, I sat in the tub, lost in thought, as the water cooled around me. My eyes drifted around the bathroom to the hair dryer tucked on a shelf beneath the sink, to the small flowery-smelling bottles of shampoo and conditioner lined in a row, and, eventually, to that circular, metal overflow face plate at the front of the bathtub, midway between the drain and the faucet.

In it was a reflection of my face, warped by the curvature of the metal. If you've ever swiped to the wrong screen of an app on your phone and accidentally fired up your front-facing camera, you probably recall the shock of seeing your own face reflected back at you. I had this same reaction to my reflection in the metal plate. I looked forlorn, tired, and, more than anything else, just totally depleted.

*I'm really not in a good place right now*, I remember thinking at the time.

For years leading up to this point, productivity—the topic I was onstage that day to speak about—had been my obsession. I had built my career, and for a large part, my life, around the subject. Even as I write these words, after embarking on the journey that became this book, it continues to be my passion, one that has evolved as I've defined the place it deserves to have in my life.

But at that moment, something else became very obvious. As important as this ever-present interest was to me, and as far as exploring it had gotten me, I had failed to define boundaries around my pursuit of productivity. I felt anxious, burnt out, and depleted, like so many others who take on too much—maybe like you have felt a time or two.

Stress had built up in my life with nowhere to go.

Snapping out of the pre-talk daydream and slowly getting up off the bed, I packed my suitcase, swapped my white dress shirt for a hoodie, put on headphones, and, probably brooding a bit, walked to the train station to begin my trek home.

On the train, I had the chance to look back even further.

## Looking Back

As I began deconstructing my situation, one thing stumped me. I had always thought that some event, like an onstage panic attack, would happen because I wasn't investing in self-care.

But I *had* been taking care of myself. I actually thought I was doing a pretty good job at it!

There is an ungodly amount of advice out there for how hardworking people can take care of themselves. Leading up to the onstage panic attack, I practiced quite a bit of it, including meditating daily (typically for thirty minutes at a time); attending silent meditation retreats once or twice a year; working out several times a week; getting massages; occasionally visiting the spa with my wife; and reading books, listening to podcasts, and even taking baths on the road—often after indulging in some delicious Indian food. Investing in self-care has served as a counterbalance to my passion for productivity, which is primarily about optimizing the benefits and contributions of work.

I thought all of this would be enough—and more than that, I considered myself lucky to be able to do it all. Not everyone has the luxury or privilege to take a weeklong vacation to disconnect from the world on a meditation retreat, or the budget for a couple of massages a month. Given all the self-care I was pouring precious time and money into, it surprised me that the low-level anxiety would have the room to metastasize into a full-fledged anxiety attack.

I realized I needed to go deeper to actually find calm. That's what would eventually set me on the journey that became this book.

Toward the end of each year, usually over the holidays, I like to reflect on the year ahead and think about what I'll want to have accomplished by the time it's over. (I use this future-past tense deliberately: I find it a fun and helpful activity to mentally fast-forward, and imagine a future that I haven't yet created for myself.) Each year I set three work-related intentions—projects I'll want to have finished, parts of my business I'll want to have grown, and other milestones I'll want to have hit. I'll also mentally hit fast-forward to think about my personal life at the end of the year, and what three things I'll want to have accomplished by the time the year is done.

This particular year, the three work intentions came easily, because they were projects I already had the ball rolling on: write an audiobook on meditation and productivity (which had a deadline); make sure the talks I gave that year were fun and helpful (they were already scheduled); and get a successful podcast up and running (because who doesn't have a podcast these days?).

And even though I also typically set three grand personal intentions, after experiencing the ill-timed panic attack, I narrowed my intentions to just one: figure out how to take care of myself, properly.

And to accomplish that, I in turn focused my thinking onto a simple question: **What did I have to do for me to experience calm and make it last?**

## A Quick Lay of the Land

At the beginning of the journey, I sought only to settle my scrambled mind. But as the project progressed, I would unexpectedly come to view productivity and calm—as well as many related ideas—very differently from how I did before. Just a few of the lessons I learned, which I'll walk you through in the chapters to come, include how:

- Calm is the *polar opposite of anxiety*.
- Our constant striving for accomplishment can ironically make us *less* productive, as it leads us over time to experience chronic stress, burnout, and anxiety.
- Most of us aren't the cause of our own burnout—and better yet, there are scientifically validated ways of overcoming burnout. There are also ways to deconstruct the phenomenon of burnout to understand your situation better, like by examining how you fare with the six "burnout factors," and minding your "burnout threshold."
- There is a common enemy of calm that we must face down in the modern world: our desire for dopamine, a neurochemical in our brain that leads us to overstimulate ourselves. Lowering our "stimulation height"—which is determined by how much dopamine-releasing stimuli we attend to on a regular basis— gets us closer to calm.

- Many sources of stress in our lives are hidden from our view, but can be fun to tame through a "stimulation detox," which is sometimes referred to as a "dopamine detox." Resetting our mind's tolerance for stimulation leads us to become calmer, less anxious, and less burnt out.
- Nearly all habits that lead us to calm exist in one place: the analog world. The more time we spend in the analog world, as opposed to the digital one, the calmer we become. We best unwind in the analog world, acting in accordance with how our ancient brain is wired.
- We can invest in our calm and productivity *at the same time*. We become far more productive when we work deliberately and with intention, not when our mind is anxiously tugged in many directions at once. There are even ways of calculating just how much time we can earn back by investing in calm.

Above any single lesson, one of the most significant mindset shifts I'd personally make relates to the last point, productivity. In an overanxious world, I would eventually come to believe that the path to greater productivity *runs straight through calm*.

By the time my own journey was said and done, I had stumbled upon countless tactics, ideas, and mindset shifts we can all adopt to find calm in our lives—even during the most hectic days.

I'll begin sharing these with you by exploring the two primary sources of modern anxiety: the "mindset of more" and our tendency to fall victim to superstimuli—highly processed, exaggerated versions of things we're naturally wired to enjoy. We'll explore how these factors influence us to both structure our lives around the neurochemical dopamine, and embrace abnormal levels of chronic stress. Where helpful,

I'll share stories from my own journey, ideas from interesting researchers I met along the way, and, of course, share practical advice to help with all of these impulses.

After exploring the factors that drive us from calm, we'll dig even deeper into how we can fill our days with calm, covering topics like how stress works, our common anxiety "escape hatches," why we shouldn't feel guilty about investing in calm, and other specific strategies we can invest in to overcome anxiety. Throughout the book, I'll also share what I learned from a bunch of experiments I tried in my own life, including compartmentalizing when and where I cared about productivity; conducting a one-month dopamine fast to try to destimulate my mind in the most extreme way possible; and resetting my tolerance to caffeine.

Let's begin this dive into calm by covering a subject near and dear to me, one that I would need to develop a healthier relationship with in order to find calm. That topic, as you might have guessed, is productivity.

Whether we're aware of it or not, the world we find ourselves in leads us to think quite a bit about how much we accomplish. As I found firsthand, this drive toward greater productivity and accomplishment can lead us to believe an incredible number of stories about ourselves—regardless of whether they're true—while taking on a significant amount of chronic stress in the process.

As soon as you're ready, let's cannonball straight into the deep end and explore what I've come to think of as the "accomplishment mindset."

CHAPTER TWO

*Striving for Accomplishment*

## Forging an Identity

It would be impossible for me to share what I've learned about calm without first talking about accomplishment—and how we construct our identities out of what we achieve. In large part, our identity is made up of the stories we believe about ourselves—as well as the stories others tell us about who we are.

If you could rewind a videotape of your life—moving in fast-reverse through the celebrations, triumphs, and challenges—you'd reach a point at which your identity hadn't formed yet. You were just a kid, absorbing the world with all the wonderment of a figurine looking up inside of a snow globe. You were also gathering evidence of yourself—stories of the world around you, and about who you believe you are. . . .

Wide-eyed, inquisitive, and with your cheek pressed against the wet, grassy ground—maybe poking at a frog with your index finger—you hear the muted background hum of your aunt talking to one of your parents about how curious a kid you are, with words not intended for you. A story begins to form in your mind:

*Am I curious? Well, I guess I am. What does this mean? . . .*

Fast-forward to high school—the first year, physics class. Physics never connected with you, but for some reason, your teacher has just . . . some perfect way of explaining how elements of the world interact with one another.

*Maybe I am scientifically minded? I mean, I've always been pretty logical. What does this say about me? . . .*

Hit fast-forward again, and push play right when you get to the week you're starting your second job. In a meeting, offhandedly, your new boss—your favorite boss still to this day—comments on how reliable you are in your first week, and how you always seem to have some magical ability to get everything that's on your plate done.

*Of course I'm reliable. That's part of who I am; I guess I'm just productive.*

Over time, memories accumulate like evidence—of who we're becoming, and eventually, of who we believe we are.

In my own story, I carried around narratives identical to these—that I was curious, logical, and productive—until I eventually embarked on a yearlong productivity project, where I researched and experimented with as much productivity advice as I possibly could. At the beginning of the project, straight out of university, I declined two full-time, well-paying jobs to make zero money for a year and explore the topic of productivity as thoroughly as possible. (In Canada, we can defer repayment of our student loans for a while, which made the project a whole lot easier.) As you might imagine, an endeavor like this had a way of reinforcing the narratives I believed about myself.

Some of the narratives that the project reinforced were true, like that I was deeply curious about the science of productivity. As weird an interest as it is, that one's still true today—maybe even more so.

But I had started to construct other narratives, like that I was some kind of superhumanly productive person. This identity was built on less stable ground, and, unfortunately for me, the more ideas and strategies I experimented with, the more evidence I saw for this particular story. This only served to make me more ensconced within it.

Of course, the stories didn't just come from me. For example, after I watched seventy hours of TED Talks in a week (to experiment with information retention), the TED Talks organization wrote that I "might be the most productive man you'd ever hope to meet." This felt pretty damn great at the time. Even if I recognized it was a little over the top, hearing the quote read back to me repeatedly in interviews and before talks was no doubt shaping the stories I told myself (not to mention my ego). With time, more complimentary quotes rolled in—fuel for the fire that would forge my newfound identity.

I knew a good amount about productivity, and like to think that I really had learned or even developed the strategies to approach my work in an intelligent way. You might *expect* that this is the case, given I've spent so much time researching, thinking about, and experimenting with the topic. Carpenters should know how to build furniture, teachers should know how to teach, productivity researchers should know how to get a good amount done in the time it would take others to do a little.

But in blindly accepting the narrative that I was *unstoppably* productive, I, like so many others, failed to account for the fact that there was a point at which I could push myself too far. I knew a lot about productivity—but there was also a lot I didn't know. Crucially, I didn't have a proper perspective on how productivity deserved to fit into the broader picture of my life.

Maybe, just maybe, I was a bit more stressed than I was letting on to myself, and constantly being on the road for work was wearing me down more than I cared to admit. And perhaps I had trapped myself in a story; one that, in practice, was impossible to live up to, and would eventually drive me to anxiety and burnout.

Ideally, in forming an identity, we pick attributes of ourselves that are stable over time, and structure our identity on top of what we most deeply value. But we often pick parts of our life that are not—including what we do for a living. Of course, as soon as our work—or anything else, for that matter—becomes a part of our identity, losing it feels like losing a piece of ourselves. I had made this same mistake: in my eyes, my work was no longer something I did, it had become a part of who I *was*. Every complimentary email from a reader, blurb from a media outlet, and kind remark became yet another piece of evidence for this narrative, another pail of wet concrete poured into the foundation of this newfound hyperproductive identity.

Burning out, falling deep into an episode of anxiety onstage, and even simpler moments like the memory of seeing myself in the bathtub plate, would insert a wedge between myself and who I believed I was, stark reminders that the evidence on which I based a large part of my identity just wasn't true.

I would be stretching the truth if I said that I realized all of this on the train ride home after the event. But one thing became apparent on that trip: I had taken my single-minded pursuit of productivity to a place where its foundation was no longer stable. Something was missing.

## The Birth of a Mindset

To help kick off the book, here's a deceptively simple question for you to reflect on: How do you determine whether a day of your life went well?

Honestly think about this question for a minute or two, in whatever way you'd like. Journal about what comes to mind, pause and reflect for a minute or two, or talk it through with your spouse or partner (a favorite technique of mine). If you're like me, you might find this question a fun one to turn over in your mind for a bit.

(I'll be here when you're done.)

If you gave the question some thought, you probably realized that there are countless ways you can measure a day—depending on the values you focus on as you answer the question. Some different answers that I've heard (along with their corresponding deeper values in parentheses) include:

- the extent to which you were able to help other people, whether personally or through your work (service);
- how many tasks you crossed off your to-do list (productivity);
- how much you were able to savor your day (enjoyment);
- how much money you made (financial success);
- how engaged you were with your work or life (presence);
- how many deep and genuine moments you shared with others (connection); and
- whether the day made you happy (happiness).

These are just a few examples. In addition to your values, how you measure your days could also be informed by elements of your life like the culture you live and work inside of, your stage of life, your upbringing, and what opportunities are available to you. Someone raised by investment banker parents is likely to evaluate their days differently than someone raised by free-spirited parents living out of a Volkswagen van.

It should be said that there is no correct answer to this question. While most of us don't step back at the end of each day to evaluate how things went—not all of us have a practice like journaling or meditation, for example—on some level, often subconscious, we do reflect on whether a day was good. As long as you've enjoyed how you've spent your time, and live in accordance with what you value, you're going to feel pretty good about how your days unfold—regardless of whether they look ruthlessly competitive or like some far-out hippie adventure to others. If you're satisfied at the end of each day, that should be enough—it's your time to spend however the heck you want.

However, despite the myriad ways we can measure how we've spent our time, or ways our values and environments differ, most of us seem to measure how well a day went by how much we were able to get done or how productive we were.

This is typically the case at work. But if you're anything like me, you may also take this attitude home with you.

## The Accomplishment Mindset

If you were to rewind the tape of your life yet again, you would hopefully find your younger self giving little thought to how productive you were, or how much you were able to accomplish in a day. Occupying fewer stories about yourself, you also thought less about what was expected of you and had fewer expectations of yourself.

If you're similar to me, your younger self was a freer spirit—following the proverbial wind, and doing things simply for the sake of doing them. Maybe you built time capsules, biked to new places, and cooked up kitchen concoctions that, while fun to make, were actually gross, sloppy mixes of flour, ketchup, and other random condiments you could reach on the kitchen shelves.

Every once in a while, maybe you even had the freedom of mind to stumble into boredom—which led you to brainstorm more novel ways to spend your time. Maybe you built a blanket fort out of the chairs and the couch in the living room, or attached all of the fruit stickers to the bottom of the wall cabinets in the kitchen. (When was the last time you were bored?)

When you were younger, you didn't give much thought to measuring your days. Of course, as we progress through life and accumulate real responsibility, this changes. We're taught to measure our time—and often even our worth—against the benchmark of accomplishment.* As adults, this weight of responsibility can drive us away from serendipitous adventure.

Even in kids, this mindset can form quickly. When we start school, we enter into a system with targets that we compete against others to achieve: the better our grades, the further we'll make it in the school system, and the further we'll make it in life. Good grades are how we become a rocket scientist, a brain surgeon, a high-flying CEO who sails the skies in a Gulfstream. The more focused we are as we work, the more resourceful we'll become, and the more driven we are, the more accomplished we'll become. We then enter the workforce with ever more immediate targets to strive for—higher salaries, performance bonuses, and rungs climbed in the organizational hierarchy above us. Regardless of how far we get, we strive for more. Such is the nature of the accomplishment mindset: once we begin shooting for more success, we tend not to stop.

As we grow up and accumulate more responsibilities, there are more options for things we can do with every minute of our time, and not all these options are created equal. Continually asking ourselves

---

\* It's probably a worthwhile reminder that your life is worth so much more than what you're able to accomplish with it.

whether there are more important alternatives to what we are doing—what an economist might call the "opportunity cost" of our time—leads us to feel guilty and doubt whether we're spending our limited, valuable time on the best possible activity. Responsibility makes how we spend our time more consequential, because it raises this opportunity cost. If the thought of going on an adventure were to pass through our mind, the very next thought might be all of the more important things we could do instead. The laundry needs to be folded. The dog needs to get walked. Emails need to be answered.

Real life gets in the way.

Even if your attention to responsibility and opportunity cost is initially limited to work, you may also reach a tipping point of sorts where your relentless focus on productivity becomes a mindset that spills into your personal life. Instead of productivity being just a set of practices to which you can turn when you have more work than time to do it, getting the most done with every moment is always on your mind—including when you actually would just like to relax.

**I call this the accomplishment mindset.** The accomplishment mindset is a conditioned set of attitudes and beliefs that drives us to constantly strive to accomplish more. This mindset leads us to always want to fill our time with something—and feel guilty when we're spending our time in a "nonoptimal" way. It's the force that tells us, when we're out enjoying a latte with a friend, that we should really go home to get a head start on dinner; the voice telling us to catch up on our podcast queue while we're relishing a beautiful walk through the park. Above all else, the mindset leads us to continually think about the opportunity cost of our time—and how we can use our limited time to achieve more.

Most of us don't evaluate our time and intentions through this mindset 100 percent of the time. But, as we move forward in our lives and careers, we seem to measure more of our hours, days, weeks, and years against the yardstick of accomplishment. Telling ourselves the story that we'll set the mindset aside when we retire, we keep on trucking.

Relaxation can wait, and so too can savoring the fruits of what we accomplish. Being an "accomplished person" can become a part of our identity. When our list of work accomplishments fuses with our personal identity, we see our success as a part of who we are.

In her book *The Writing Life*, Annie Dillard makes the case that how we spend our days is how we spend our lives. I would extend this to how we *measure* our days, too: how we measure our days is how we measure our lives. When we measure our days by how much we're able to accomplish in them, and we're not careful, we measure the sum of our days this way, too.

School and work can make us care a bit too much about productivity and accomplishment, but they obviously serve an important purpose. They have built the modern world as we know it.

It's hard to overstate just how much better off we are in the modern world. If you took a farm laborer from two hundred years ago and brought him to a nice grocery store, he probably would not be able to process just how bountiful it is. And grocery stores are nowhere *near* the most luxurious trappings of modern life. Once the poor guy calms down (which might take a while), you could very slowly pull your phone out of your pocket and show him how the device lets you connect with anyone on earth, at any moment, in under one second.

Thanks to economic progress, over the last two hundred years, the average American's yearly income has gone from $2,000 a person to $50,000—and that's *after* accounting for inflation. And while we've become *twenty-five times* more affluent, the price of many goods has also come down, in large part due to technological progress. The $1,000 that you spent on a TV eighty years ago gets you a lot more inches and pixels today. And it'll even be in color!

As you would hope, it's not just those of us in wealthier countries that benefit from this growth. Over the last two decades, the number of people living in extreme poverty around the world has more than *halved*. Twenty years ago, 29 percent of the world lived in extreme poverty. Today, 9 percent do. Economic indicators like these matter a lot. As renowned researcher Hans Rosling wrote in *Factfulness*, "The main factor that affects how people live is not their religion, their culture, or the country they live in, but their income."

For all of these reasons, I am not about to make the case against economic growth, which, assuming the benefits are spread fairly among us (a strong assumption), truly does make our lives better.

But this modern world has come with a price: anxiety. The systems we live and work inside of—and the mindsets they lead us to adopt and the stress they lead us to take on—are significant contributors to this. Productivity and accomplishment are incentivized whether we're at school or work. In the long arc of time, the more productive we are, the more "successful" we tend to become.

Modern society places a high prize on traditional measures of success, like money, status, and recognition—ignoring less quantifiable measures, like how happy we are, how deep and fulfilling our relationships are, and whether we make a difference in the lives of others. And the way we get to become more accomplished is through becoming more productive, accumulating enough productive days that they lead to an "accomplished" life. As we spend more time in systems that reward productivity, we become convinced that productivity and accomplishment are what matter most.

Eventually, this becomes the default way we measure how well we've spent our time.

## The Wonders of Productivity Advice

In this chapter, I've focused primarily on the costs of striving for productivity at the expense of your well-being, but there are great benefits to be had, too, especially when you give your productivity practice boundaries.

If the mental image the word "productivity" conjures up for you feels cold, corporate, and all about efficiency, you're not alone. But you need not worry. There are far friendlier approaches to the subject, and productivity advice doesn't have to turn you into a robot addicted to accomplishment.

I view productivity as simply accomplishing what we set out to do—whether our intention is to clear all the emails from our inbox, decide between a few candidates to hire onto our team at work, or relax on a beach while drinking two piña coladas (one for each hand). In my eyes, when we set out to do something, and then do it, we're perfectly productive. Framed a different way, productivity is not about striving for more—it's about intention. This definition works across every context, regardless of what area of our life we're operating in.

But even with this (hopefully more human) definition, productivity and accomplishment are two sides of the same coin, even when what we intend to "accomplish" is a day of relaxation. I'll set aside this friendlier definition for a moment because it's worth evaluating the pursuit of accomplishment using a more traditionally accepted definition of the term: making progress toward our goals and accomplishments (to become more successful by traditional measures).

Productivity tactics are neither good nor bad. Methods, habits, and strategies that lead us to become more accomplished can be deployed for incredible purposes. I found this firsthand: productivity is one of my favorite topics in the world, and focusing on it has led me to create a substantial amount of work that I am proud of, a degree of success I probably would not have achieved otherwise. But at the same time, this focus on accomplishment has driven me to burnout and anxiety.

In the productivity space, the idea that striving for more accomplishment can lead to both success and harm is rarely discussed, if at all.

So let's talk about it.

For good reason, the draw of productivity advice is difficult to resist. Every single day, there are things that we need to get done, at work and at home. We live big lives, filled to the brim with responsibility. In one day, we might have ten hours of work to get done (in eight), while working from home with a sick kid in the other room, while somehow finding time to pay the overdue bills piling up in our email inbox. On another day—maybe even on the weekend!—we may need to catch up on chores around the house, while cooking dinner for our extended family, while hopefully scraping together enough time to properly unwind.

Productivity advice works remarkably well in situations like these. The productivity advice that actually works more than pays for itself— we make back the time we spend on it *and then some*. By accomplishing what we have to do in less time, we carve out more time for what's meaningful—people, hobbies, and work we can connect with on a deeper level.

As a simple example, take prioritizing the tasks that comprise your workday. By spending just a few minutes at the start of each day defining what you'll want to have accomplished by the day's end, you figure out what your most valuable tasks are, and in the process understand where your time is best spent and where it isn't. Just a few minutes of planning can save you *hours* in execution later on, especially if doing so helps you zero in on your most essential tasks on a given day, or stop working on a project that would be better delegated to someone else on your team.

Imagine, for a second, that you've won some one-in-a-million contest through a high-end housecleaning service that provides you with a full-time butler for life. (His name is Kingsley.) The man provides you with more free time every day, by cleaning up after you and your family, cooking meals, managing your calendar (which he calls your "diary"), chauffeuring you around town, and more. The best part: Kingsley's handsome salary is paid, in full, until his retirement, fifty years from today. You don't even have to tip him (that's included)! While this scenario is sadly a pipe dream for nearly all of us, the best productivity tactics and strategies can confer similar benefits. Like Kingsley, they provide us with more of the most valuable resource we have at our disposal: time.

This is the promise, and wonder, of productivity advice. By developing your capacity to get things done, you have more time, attention, and energy to bring to everything that you do. You might even become more successful to boot.

But unlike with a butler, this advice should come with an important caveat: it's helpful *provided we at some point stop our striving.* Productivity advice is powerful, but it requires boundaries.

Without them, this obsession with accomplishment can diminish our productivity, because it drives us away from calm.

## The Opposite of Calm

A few months after my panic attack, work finally slowed a bit and I could begin deconstructing what had made me so anxious and burnt out. I'll get to the science of burnout in the next chapter, but first let's decipher what it even means to be *calm*—the end result that we're after.

Researchers, I quickly discovered, do not study calm as a standalone construct. Most of us know what calm *feels* like, and its definition is right there in the dictionary—smack-dab between "callus" and "calomel"—with descriptions such as "a quiet and peaceful state or condition" and "without hurried movement, anxiety, or noise." But the term does not have a commonly agreed-upon clinical definition. Few, if any, have even been suggested. Calm is also not a branch of psychology that is studied, nor is there a validated, reliable instrument designed to precisely assess how calm someone is. (After many hours of scouring various academic search engines, I was happy to have finally found the Vancouver Inter-action and Calmness Scale. In this scale, however, "calmness" refers to how sedate a patient receiving mechanical ventilation is in the ICU—including whether they're pulling out their lines or tubes!)

Forget how elusive calm is in everyday life. It's even elusive in the research!

Thankfully, there is a way we can circumvent this lack of an official, clinical definition, while staying true to the research. We can do this through exploring anxiety. While research regarding calm is very scarce, the research that does exist points to a curious idea: calm is *the polar opposite of anxiety*. We can begin to form our own definition of calm by exploring its opposite.

When we're anxious, we feel inner turmoil; ruminating, while filled with dread about what's to come. Research suggests that we may also feel nervous or on edge during anxious periods, while unable to stop our worrying. Other signs of anxiety include having trouble relaxing, feeling restless, annoyed or irritable, and frequently afraid, as if something terrible might happen at any moment. I think of my own anxiety as a sort of rolling impatience, where anxious moments of the day crash into each other like waves.

Calm is the opposite of all this turmoil. Luckily for us, research provides insight into exactly how the states differ. Importantly, while anxiousness is an *unpleasant* emotion characterized as a state of *high* mental arousal, calm is a *pleasant* emotion characterized as a state of *low* mental arousal.

Research has confirmed that calm and anxiety exist on a continuum with one another, with one recent study published in the American Psychological Association's renowned *Journal of Personality and Social Psychology* demonstrating that anxiety doesn't go from "zero to intense" as we think, but should instead be thought of as a *continuum* that ranges "from high calmness to high anxiety":

High Calmness                 High Anxiety

Put differently, calm isn't just the polar opposite of anxiety—anxiety is the polar opposite of calm. Not only does overcoming anxiety get us closer to calm, but when we foster high levels of calm in our life, we have further to go before we become anxious again. Calmness makes us resilient against future anxiety.

Taking these findings together, we can define calm as *a subjectively positive state characterized by a low level of arousal, with an accompanying absence of anxiety.* As we move away from the High Anxiety side of the spectrum toward High Calmness, our feelings of contentedness grow deeper as our mind becomes more relaxed and serene. Eventually, with our thoughts still and our mind settled, we experience calm. In this state, we are also less emotionally reactive to the events of our life.

It should be said that we don't always experience anxiety and calm in the same way. Our subjective state is continually in flux. For this reason (and with the assumption you do not suffer from an anxiety disorder, which I cover briefly in the box below), we should be thinking about anxiety and calm not as *traits* we have, but rather as *states* we pass through, depending on factors such as what's happening in our lives and how much stress we're under at a given time. Anxiety is a normal response to a stressful situation, especially one we interpret as threatening. There's nothing wrong with you if you experience it.

Some days are full of calm but contain an anxious moment or two—like when our airport shuttle arrives to pick us up thirty minutes late. On the flip side, days full of anxious moments might be punctuated by refreshing periods of calm—like when the stress of work evaporates the moment we walk in the front door at home, and our kids run to hug us at our knees.

This path to calm—which involves reducing anxiety but also investing in strategies that get us to the *other* end of the calm spectrum—is one in which we'll eliminate stress, overcome burnout, and resist distraction, while becoming more engaged, present, and productive.

Before going any further, I should put on my legal hat (it's like my regular hat, but it charges me by the hour), and mention that the advice in this book should not be construed, and is not intended to serve, as a substitute for advice from a trained medical professional. You should absolutely consult with a doctor if you are experiencing levels of anxiety that are preventing you from functioning in your day-to-day life, or in any way make your mind feel like an unpleasant place to spend time. If you're curious about whether you might have an anxiety disorder—also called *trait* anxiety, as opposed to *state* anxiety—and you *don't* want to speak to a professional, I highly recommend searching for the Generalized Anxiety Disorder 7. This free test, which is available online, serves as a screener for generalized anxiety disorder. It's just seven short questions, takes a minute or two to answer, and will ask you how often you experience anxiety symptoms like the ones I mentioned a few paragraphs ago—which I've adapted directly from this test. The bottom line: get help if you need it—or even if you just think you might! My intention with this book is to help with the low-level subclinical anxiety that so many of us experience, especially in the modern accomplishment-obsessed world.

## The Productivity Spectrum

Now that we've defined calm, let's get back to productivity and accomplishment. As with calm and anxiety, we all fall on a spectrum of sorts with regard to how highly we value and think about productivity and accomplishment.

On one end of the spectrum is the person who never thinks about productivity or what they want to accomplish with their time. This isn't ideal. An obsessive pursuit of productivity can negatively affect our mental health, but we do need to set and then work toward a few goals. We should probably try to earn a livable paycheck, help those around us, and live in a way that will minimize our future regret (in my opinion, minimizing regret is one of the most important ingredients of a good life). Someone who never thinks about what they want to get out of their time rarely sets out to make their life better, or live in a way that's congruent with what they value. We've got to spend at least *some* of our time working toward our goals. Plus, our mind craves having things to engage with throughout the day. (Engagement makes us happier than almost any other ingredient in our life—more on this later.)

On the opposite end of the spectrum is someone who is constantly driven by an accomplishment mindset, and values accomplishment and productivity above all else—including other great ingredients that make up a good life, like happiness, connection, and calm. For this person, productivity is basically a religion that they practice at work and in all parts of their lives. As productivity and accomplishment became tangled up with the stories that made up my identity, I moved close to that end of the spectrum. If stories about your own success have become entangled with your identity, or you find it difficult to set the accomplishment mindset aside, including when you want to relax, perhaps you've moved on over to this side of the spectrum, too.

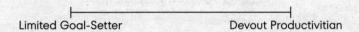

Limited Goal-Setter                    Devout Productivitian

When achievement drives most of what we do, we run the risk of not taking time to recharge, slow down, or appreciate the fruits of what we accomplish—all of which, ironically, make us more motivated and productive in the long run. We need to spend at least some of our time refueling, or we run the risk of burning out.

Reflect on where you fall on the spectrum, particularly if you care about productivity and accomplishment more than most. As it relates to calm, the accomplishment mindset can be a double-edged sword when we take it too far: it leads us to less joy, while causing us more stress.

Let's cover each of these ideas in turn.

## Less Joy

An early discovery I made in my quest for calm was the extent to which the accomplishment mindset inhibited how much joy I experienced each day. The reason for this was simple: the mindset turned pretty much everything in my life into a to-do item. As the saying goes, when the only tool you have is a hammer, every problem looks like a nail. A similar idea rings true here: when you see everything you do through the lens of the accomplishment mindset, everything in your life looks like something you have to get done. In this way, an accomplishment mindset compromises how much joy you experience each day, as you alternate between periods of productivity, as well as guilt (when you're not being productive).*

I found this from firsthand experience. Instead of savoring delicious meals, I ate them while distractedly listening to a podcast or watching a YouTube video, in a two-pronged attempt to both fit more into that time, while trying to absolve myself of the guilt I felt taking a break (a subject we'll dig in to in chapter 8). I chose busyness over genuine enjoyment, stubbornly and repeatedly. When I had scheduled a conversation with a friend at the end of the day, I couldn't escape the shackles of the mindset then, either, thinking about what I had to get done when

---

* This is not to say that we shouldn't value our time highly, or consider the opportunity cost of our time to make sure we spend it on valuable things. Time is the most limited resource we have with which to live a good life. We should value it highly. In fact, we should value our time so highly that we don't just try to use the time to get stuff done.

I got back to work the next day. As I became unusually concerned with how productive I was, I'm sad to say that even the most enjoyable activities in my life—time with my wife, meals, and other incredible experiences—became to-do items. Even vacations became something to get done, rather than enjoy.

Productivity became the end I was seeking. Of course, productivity is a terrible end in and of itself: it should be thought of as *a means to a more important end*, such as having more free time, financial freedom, or more space to genuinely connect with others.*

As many of us do, I lived life at capacity, with little slack or free time in my schedule. At least, this was the story I had convinced myself of. It turns out I did have the time—I just wasn't spending it on activities that made me engaged or calm. Each time I hit a productivity milestone, the accomplishment mindset took over once again, and I focused on the next thing I needed to get done, never fully appreciating that I had achieved the last thing.

An accomplishment mindset is nice to have when we're at work, on company time. Work is how we exchange our time for money. We are paid for our productivity over an arc of time, assuming things are fair. Productivity leads to micro-accomplishments, which lead to more substantial achievement. But when we're not careful, the same mindset that leads us to achievement at work can prevent us from enjoying the best parts of our life when we're *not* trading our time for money. Instead of enjoying moments, we tick boxes, all while spending less time savoring the fruits of our accomplishments—the vacations, the two-story house,

---

* A related, secondary cost of the accomplishment mindset is how it feeds our individualism, which leads us to think less about others. The mindset leads us to think primarily about ourselves: it's about how productive *we* are, not how much we can help other people, how productive our team is, or the life we're able to create with our loved ones. A lesson I'm continually relearning is that I have a near-unlimited amount of space inside me to welcome in other people.

the quality time with family—the things we work so hard for in the first place.

If you lose sight of this, as I did, you may also find that *everything becomes work*—something you need to do to get a result. Your to-do list becomes a diary of stuff you *have* to do, not things you *get* to do.

It's surprisingly easy to bully yourself into becoming a more productive person. After all, it's impossible to want to improve your life without first deciding how you don't quite measure up to others. This is what can make self-improvement a trap, especially when you take the accomplishment mindset to the most extreme.*

Unlike me, you hopefully haven't moved this far to the end of the productivity spectrum. But the point stands regardless: without boundaries, the accomplishment mindset leads us to experience less joy, especially when it's time to relax.

When we're striving for accomplishment all of the time, we never truly enjoy where we are, what we're doing, or, most important, whom we get to do it all with.

## A Mirage of Productivity

A second cost of the accomplishment mindset is one I've already alluded to: it leads us to become needlessly busy, especially with small, unimportant tasks, because it pushes us to fill each moment of our lives to the brim with activity. This busyness is often just a signal we send to the evaluating part of our mind that we're moving forward toward our intended accomplishments—even if we're just bouncing between apps,

---

* As a general rule, it's worth spending less time trying to improve yourself, and more time becoming happy with yourself.

scrolling past social media updates, or impulsively reading the news. We feel less guilty engaging in mindless scrolling than when resting and recharging—even though doing so saps our energy, and stresses us out.

Some busyness is obviously just a fact of life, and a result of our accumulating meaningful responsibility—but at the same time, the era of pocketable internet devices has introduced a whole new and unnecessary layer of busyness to our day. Just a couple of decades ago, this layer of activity didn't exist! Today, when we have a few minutes to spare between meetings, we tend to focus on things that keep our minds stimulated instead of planning what we want to get out of our time. Refreshing our email one more time, rechecking Instagram, or doomscrolling our way around Twitter, we feel busy—and this busyness tricks our mind into thinking we're accomplishing something. But it's really just a mirage of productivity.

Unfortunately, this busyness also drives us from calm, because it leads us to take on more chronic stress than is necessary.* As I delved deeper into the research surrounding anxiety and calm, eliminating sources of chronic stress in my life—a great number of which stemmed from this unnecessary busyness layer brought on by the achievement-driven mindset—led to the best progress I made in achieving greater calm. I cannot underscore this point enough: chronic stress, much of which stems from the accomplishment mindset, is perhaps the largest roadblock you'll need to tackle to achieve lasting mental calm.

Let me explain.

In a nutshell, we experience two flavors of stress in our life. The first kind, *acute* stress, is stress that is temporary and often one-off—one

---

* Also ironically, an accomplishment mindset can lead us to waste more time: faced with some unexpected downtime, we squander it, surfing social media and tapping around on rectangular screens, because we feel guilty about indulging in genuinely rewarding relaxation. It's always easier to choose busyness.

rebooked flight, a Lego block that we step on in the middle of the night, or an argument with our spouse that's finally resolved. Thankfully for us, our bodies are *designed* to deal with acute stress—for most of human history, acute stress was the primary type of stress we've experienced. We human beings were nothing more than delicious prey for millions of years, devoured by leopards, snakes, and giant hyenas. Our body's stress response provided us with the physical and mental stamina to face down threats like these.

Acute stress is, by its very definition, short-term and temporary. You may be familiar with how your body responds to episodes of acute stress: it releases cortisol, a stress hormone, which activates your body's stress response. This stress response provides us with the mental and physical stamina we need to fight back against whatever happens to be stressing us, so we can get on with our lives. Your body floods with adrenaline, your pupils dilate, and you either run away, or slay that killer hyena like the badass that you are.

Stress gets a bad rap, but unfairly so. The truth is more nuanced: stress isn't fun while we experience it, but it gives our life meaning. Acute stress is akin to a tunnel we must navigate through to arrive at a better place on the other side. Great memories are often the result of experiences that feel stressful in the moment. Weddings are stressful. So is cooking a weekend dinner for your extended family. So is speaking about your work in front of a hundred people. But experiences like these are what *make life meaningful*. As psychologist Kelly McGonigal so eloquently put it in her book *The Upside of Stress*, "If you put a wider lens on your life and subtract every day that you have experienced as stressful, you won't find yourself with an ideal life. Instead, you'll find yourself also subtracting the experiences that have helped you grow, the challenges you are most proud of, and the relationships that define you."

Acute stress provides us with memories to look back on, experiences that end up feeling rich, and challenges from which we have little choice but to grow.

"Chronic" stress, though, is the opposite. It's the no good, very bad type of stress that feels like it's never going to end and that we face over and over again—chronically. Instead of the one-time canceled flight, it's the grueling traffic we encounter every damn day on our way to work. Instead of the occasional argument with our spouse, it's the irreconcilable feelings that arise whenever we talk to them.

There is an end in sight with acute stress, even when the stress is at its peak. Our body has a chance to recover after we've passed through the stressful experience. The same thing cannot be said about chronic stress.

Unfortunately for us, in the modern, accomplishment-driven world, sources of chronic stress are endless. Some of them are even hidden—the result of our unnecessary busyness.

Many sources of chronic stress are easy to spot: struggling financially to make ends meet, dealing with constant negativity from our annoying coworkers, and having to care for ailing family members are all experiences that don't let up and that cause us strain.

But other sources of chronic stress are hidden. We often even *choose* to pay attention to these sources of stress because they stimulate our mind to feel productive. Some of this stress is even *addictive*, because it's stimulating or provides us with validation—despite the fact that, on some level, our mind appraises the stimuli as threatening. For example, you may find that Twitter is stimulating and addictive—but think also about how your mind is invariably shaken up after using it. Or you may find that, while Instagram is equally stimulating, you feel inadequate after spending time in the app, because, as Facebook whistleblower Frances Haugen put it in her congressional testimony, the app is about two things: bodies and comparing lifestyles. Social media is full of content that makes us feel inadequate and causes us unnecessary stress.

Many, if not most of our largest sources of *distraction* are also sources of chronic stress. This is particularly true during anxious times, when a higher proportion of the distracting content we consume is threatening.

As stimulating as email, social media, and the news can be, we often pay attention to these objects of attention *because* they're stressful—not to mention novel and threatening. Many of these stressful websites and apps also provide variable reinforcement—which means sometimes there's something new and stimulating to check out, and sometimes there isn't. This makes these sources of chronic stress addictive. Stress can also be addictive because it's familiar, like a toxic relationship we've grown comfortable inside of, which would leave an odd-shaped hole in our life if it were gone.

The news is a terrific example of a stressor that we've grown accustomed to being stressed out by, especially in recent years. Though we consume the news by choice, usually to stay informed, doing so leads us to become far more stressed than we might realize. Ironically, this provides us with a diminished mental capacity to deal with news stories directly affecting us and those we love. One study found that participants who watched six or more hours of news coverage about the Boston Marathon bombings experienced a higher level of stress than someone *in the marathon* who was directly affected by it. Another study found that watching wall-to-wall coverage of domestic terrorist attacks led viewers to develop symptoms of post-traumatic stress disorder. Worse yet, watching negative news has been shown to lead viewers to consume yet more threatening content in the future, fueling what some researchers call "a cycle of distress." If you read and watch a lot of news, let research like this give you pause. This applies to other sources of distraction, too: just because something stimulates your mind does not mean that it makes you happy or that it's not stressful or threatening. The opposite is often the case. Drinking a delicious cup of coffee, we might exhale a relaxed *aah* after taking the first sip. We never do the same after checking social media.

Unfortunately, our body cannot distinguish between acute and chronic stress: it mobilizes in the same way for both.

Like a parachute, our body's stress response is designed for only occasional use. Over millions of years, the system was designed to help us mobilize so we can overcome occasional, substantial, life-threatening stressors—and glide back to earth afterward.

Our desire for busyness, driven by the accomplishment mindset, can cost us when we're not careful. We must rein the mindset in—even when accomplishment is what we seek in the first place.

So how can we do so?

To end the chapter, let's cover two helpful strategies for reducing the costs associated with the mindset and the stories we tell ourselves about productivity. These strategies can help us move away from the extreme polar ends of the productivity spectrum, leading us to experience less stress and more joy—while leading us to greater calm.

The two strategies: define your "productivity hours" and create a "stress inventory." Let's cover each of these in turn.[*]

## Productivity Hours

The accomplishment mindset needs boundaries—without them, it tends to take over your life. (We'll cover reasons it does in chapter 4.)

---

[*] As you'll find, chronic stress is a topic that winds its way through the rest of the book. We won't deal with it all in this chapter—some sources of it are addictive, hard to get rid of, or deeply embedded in our daily routine—but we'll start to make a good dent now.

After realizing that I filtered most moments of every day through the lens of becoming as productive as possible, I started to carve out time to purposefully *not* care about productivity or accomplishment—and set up those boundaries. This way, I could get work done within the hours I chose, while making time for some much-needed calm. This went against basically every instinct I had developed studying productivity. But defining hours to not care about productivity or accomplishment worked surprisingly well. Actually, I take that back: I was *shocked* by how well it worked.

Ever since, at the start of each day, I've defined my productivity hours. Simply put, this time is when you do your work—whether office work or housework. (I find it helpful to define hours for both so I can create boundaries at work and at home, but your system may vary.) During these hours, the idea is to work on stuff you have to do that has some time pressure associated with it. You adopt the accomplishment mindset in these hours—spending time on your most valuable tasks, while finishing what you can. How many hours you need depends on factors like how many demands you have on a given day, how honed your productivity practice is, and whether or not you have a personal butler who follows you around wherever you go. The more highly you value traditional measures of accomplishment, the more productivity hours it would be worth devoting to your work each day.

Implementing this tactic is simple enough. To define these hours, at the start of each day (or at the end of the previous), examine what you have on your proverbial plate—how many meetings you have and when they occur, how much work you have to get done, and how many things you have to do around the house—and choose the hours of the day when you'll do this work. If you have an inflexible nine-to-five job, your hours should probably include your entire workday (minus lunch and other breaks).

Of course, you'll have some productivity time where you accomplish nothing at all, even though you'd *like* to, maybe because, for example, you're stuck in tedious meetings that you really don't need to be in. But here's the key: if you had the choice to skip the meetings and work more directly toward accomplishing your goals during that time, you would, because you've adopted the accomplishment mindset.

Productivity hours are a helpful tactic for dealing with the stress of work because they dictate that there is some end in sight—even during those times when you're totally swamped and have only an hour or two of personal freedom in the evening. Luckily, because you've chosen that you'll step back from work during this free time, productivity guilt is far less likely to creep in. You can compartmentalize the stories, the stress, the work anxiety—and the accomplishment mindset—while carving out some real leisure time in the process. Even during hectic periods, when it may make more sense to define your *free* hours (rather than your productivity hours), you'll create a little pocket of time to not worry about getting stuff done. Guilt and chronic work stress won't bleed into this time, especially after you've made a habit out of keeping this time strictly personal.

There's also what can be thought of as a "deadline effect" with productivity hours. When you give yourself a limited amount of time to get anything done—a deadline, in other words—you have no choice but to hunker down and act like some Devout Productivitian. As you get better at figuring out how many hours you need, you will likely surprise yourself by how much you're able to get done. Deploying this tactic will likely free up a surprising amount of time for you.

I've found it fun to use these productive hours for deliberate skill development, too—including learning photography, new programming languages, and how to play the piano (which I'm still terrible at). You don't have to be too intense about it; relax, unwind, and get stuff done. Remember that productivity doesn't have to be overly stressful, especially when you work calmly. Generally, concern yourself more with your direction than with your speed. Thoughtful deliberateness trumps directionless hustle, and what you lose in speed, you'll more than make up for in deliberateness.

Over time, be sure to make an effort to use productivity hours to focus on increasingly important tasks at work and at home. Your phone, social media, and other distractions will always await you on the other side of these hours—these hours are for working on things that lead you to keep up and make progress. If you're doing knowledge work, be sure to work a bit more slowly than you think you should, and devote plenty of time for reflection—two crucial productivity factors for doing work with your mind that let you work more strategically and less reactively. You will probably find that working more slowly saves you time in the end.

When accomplishment matters, focus on productivity. When meaning matters, be sure to set productivity aside.

Obviously, do calibrate this advice for the kind of work you do and the life you live: if you're a sales representative, you may need to connect more often in the evening than if you're a novelist. But, when work imposes itself unavoidably on your personal hours, batch together small tasks to trade in the chronic stress of ongoing distraction for the acute but contained stress of work.

Another powerful reason these hours work is that it's worse to always be *kind of* working than to work extra hours during which you're focused and productive. Blocks of focused work lead to engagement, which makes us feel like there's a purpose behind what we're doing. Conversely, spasmodically checking work email all day long leads to needless chronic stress. If you don't get paid extra to be on call, consider whether you need to be, especially if work is a significant source of chronic stress for you. Do this regardless of how needed your work makes you feel.

Use your leisure time to relax, connect, unwind, and find calm, perhaps by filling your time with a few ideas from chapter 7. During these hours, step back from what makes you feel anxious. Don't worry about output, productivity, results, or cramming more into your time. This is time for you to benefit from the fruits of your productivity, not add to your lists of accomplishments. Maybe enjoy something on your savor list (an idea from chapter 4).

Guilt is a form of internal tension, and at work it's often our brain's way of telling us that we should be working on something else—that we should consider the opportunity cost of our time. If you're not used to disconnecting intentionally, guilt will arise during this leisure time, especially as you settle into a rhythm of taking this time each day. This is normal: just notice the guilt, and try a strategy or two from later in the book (chapter 8) to keep guilt from ruining your leisure time. Guilt will arise during your productivity time, too. When it does, consider whether you're working with intention, and on the best possible thing.

If you decide to try this tactic of defining your productivity hours on for size, I hope you find what I did: that productivity hours compartmentalize the stress of work, while carving out time for joy.

If you're looking to get even more out of this time, here are a few more tips I've found helpful:

- **Remember that understanding how many productivity hours you'll need every day takes time.** You're almost guaranteed to not get it right at first and to give yourself way too many and then too few hours. But, over time, you'll become more aware of your daily capacity for accomplishment. If you're struggling with how many hours you should set aside, reflect on things like how many tasks are on your list for the day, how many meetings you have, how worn out you feel, how much energy you have, and how long you think the tasks on your plate will take to complete.

- **Try to maintain a bit of space between entering into productivity mode for work and home and family life.** This lets you transition from one role in your life (being a leader, mentor, manager, problem solver, executive, or student) to another (being a parent, grandparent, friend, or role model).

- **Keep a "later list" for when you're in leisure mode.** Or, at the very least, capture the to-dos and work ideas that come up somewhere so you can put them out of mind, yet still take advantage of them later. Remember: the less often you switch between the two modes, the more deeply you'll be able to both work and relax.

- **Be religious about stopping at the end of your productivity window of time.** It can be helpful to set an alarm for one hour before the hours end. Oddly enough, it can also be helpful to stop working in the middle of a task, because your mind will continue subconsciously thinking about it until tomorrow. Experiment to find what works for you.

- **Try to limit your switches between the two modes.** The fewer times you switch between productivity mode and leisure mode, the less mental whiplash you'll experience from constantly switching back and forth—and you'll feel more in control of your day as a result. Remember also that it's okay to ease into productivity mode. It might take you several minutes to switch from one task to the next, or to start working in the first place, and that's okay. Normal, even.

- **Be flexible if you're on a roll when you reach the end of your productivity hours and want to keep working.** Consider treating yourself: if you have a flexible work schedule, try working fewer hours the day after you get an inordinate amount of work done. Another way to treat yourself (again, if you have a flexible schedule) is to work fewer productivity hours on days when you work on a lot of tasks you've been procrastinating on.

- **Don't enter into productivity mode first thing in the morning.** Please, I beg of you. Wake up slowly, ease into the day, and reflect on what you want to get out of it. Hardly anything will make you feel less in control than checking your email immediately after sleep. Slow mornings lead to deliberate days.

- **At home, try focus sprints.** If you have a few chores to do, try setting a timer on your watch or smart speaker for fifteen minutes and challenge yourself to get as many dishes done (or [insert item here]) as possible. A short burst of fifteen minutes of chores around the house can accomplish as much as thirty to forty-five minutes of fragmented activity. I've found that the key with these smaller blocks of time is to not become too rigid about interruptions. It's okay to be interrupted, especially by people you love. Remember: people are the reason for productivity. Don't forget that when your kid or your spouse needs a hug.

Productivity hours, and the structure they provide, are a great way to define boundaries around work every day. And better yet, over time they'll lead you to make more progress toward your goals.

The art of productivity is knowing when we should care about productivity in the first place.

## The Stress Inventory

On top of containing the accomplishment mindset within your productivity hours, it's worth writing down a list of stresses you face in your life—whether those sources of stress are chronic or acute. This is the second strategy to add to your tool belt, which has the added benefit of being a helpful list to refer back to as you read this book.

Here's the challenge: take out a sheet of paper, and list everything in your life that is stressing you out. **Do not leave anything out.** Think through your entire day: look through your morning routine to your work (which may be worth dedicating an entire separate page to) and your responsibilities in your personal life. Don't worry about which sources are chronic or acute, large or small; which stressors you should probably just suck up; which ones you've been meaning to deal with. Get it all out of your head and onto the sheet of paper. Remember also to broaden your definition of stress, and include many of the distractions you tend to that serve as small but hidden sources of stress.

Seeing all of the forms of stress you face in front of you lets you step back from it all—even if you perceive some of those sources as positive.

Once you've captured the stressors you face, sort everything into a sheet with two columns on it: one for the sources of stress you can prevent, the other for ones you cannot.* Before you do this step, a word of

---

* Most sources of chronic stress are preventable if you're extreme enough about preventing them. It's possible to cancel out the stress of owning a home by moving to a rental, just as it's possible to eliminate all relationship stress from your life by becoming a hermit. If work stresses you out, you could also give up all of your earthly possessions to become a monk. Obviously, just because you can eliminate a source of stress doesn't

warning: your sources of unpreventable stress will likely outnumber what's preventable. That's normal and to be expected.

## Dealing with Low-Hanging Fruit

Stress makes us feel busy, and busyness makes us feel productive and important. But in this way, living with the accomplishment mindset can make us unnecessarily stressed. This is what makes the exercise I've just covered helpful: you can step back from the stress in your life to see how much of it is actually necessary.

In conducting this activity myself, I was surprised by just how many preventable sources of stress I faced—especially sources of chronic stress. Examples included:

- **news websites**, which constantly exposed me to information my mind perceived as a threat but that I felt compelled to check anyway;
- **nightly news broadcasts**, which left me anxious right before going to bed;
- **unnecessary email refreshes**—where I would encounter stressful fires to put out and new tasks to get done;
- one **toxic relationship** that was affecting my stress levels, which I engaged with regularly;
- **performance metrics** I would refresh regularly—podcast downloads, website visitors, and book sales—which made me feel ei-

---

mean that you should—sometimes, eliminating stress leads to more stress than what you started with, because the meaning these stressors bring to your life gets eliminated along with them. In sorting your lists, just be realistic with what's easy and what's difficult to tame, while keeping in mind that most stressors are possible to tame if you try hard enough.

ther elated or depressed, depending on the numbers that day (or hour);

- two **consulting clients** that provided me with far more stress than the others combined;

- **Twitter**, which gave me a steady stream of negative, anger-inducing updates; and

- **Instagram**, which showed me things to be envious of and inbox messages to get through, blended in with more novel images that kept me hooked.

Depending on how entrenched a source of stress is in your life, taming it can require quite a bit of work. It isn't always as simple as deleting your Facebook account—though I have yet to meet someone who regrets doing so. Coming up with a plan to eliminate a toxic relationship will probably prove more difficult than dealing with the mental stress you face from having a cluttered house. Similarly, finding a way off the work project that causes the majority of your work stress may prove more difficult than stepping back from an unimportant after-work club.

You're likely to have resistance to this activity. But if you're serious about finding calm, I'd encourage you not to bypass it. This resistance is part of the process. And as I'll get to in the next chapter, chronic stress can be far costlier than you think.

dealt with my own preventable sources of stress in turn. I replaced news websites and broadcasts with a subscription to the morning paper—trading in news sources that refreshed every five minutes for an analog briefing that refreshed once a day. I made sure to always have a specific and meaningful reason for checking social media accounts. With email,

I limited myself to one check a day outside of productivity hours (that I batched with other small tasks that came up).

Advice like this is far easier to give than it is to implement. But if you're feeling stressed, anxious, or burnt out, you need to eliminate preventable sources of chronic stress from your life. Take your pick from the list you came up with, but do tackle a few. If this is tough right now, don't worry: I'll provide you with additional strategies for doing so in the chapters to come. For now, do what you can.

Even when a source of chronic stress is difficult to eliminate—whether because you've grown accustomed to it or would find it complicated to remove from your life—doing so is almost always worthwhile. Every source of negative chronic stress you cut from your life is one less fake feeling of productivity that's cluttering up the time set aside for real accomplishment, and one less contributor to burnout, which we'll turn to in the next chapter.

As I found firsthand, burnout is something you should never have to face. Much like the accomplishment mindset, it also drives us away from calm.

CHAPTER THREE

## *The Burnout Equation*

## Unresponsive to Stress

If, after reading that last chapter, you're still in need of an extra push to tame the unnecessary chronic stress in your life, here's a lesson that I learned the hard way: the ultimate result of chronic stress is burnout. As the World Health Organization defines it in its *International Classification of Diseases,* burnout is the direct result of "chronic workplace stress that has not been successfully managed."*

It is impossible to experience burnout without first experiencing unrelenting chronic stress. This is what makes dealing with your preventable sources of chronic stress critical, even if you have to grasp at opportunities to do so or your mind resists the process. Because otherwise, burnout awaits.

As I mentioned in the previous chapter, each time we encounter a stressful situation, our body activates its stress response, unleashing cortisol, the stress hormone, on our body and mind. The intensity of this stress response depends on two things: how long we're exposed to the

---

* The World Health Organization defines burnout as a strictly workplace phenomenon. That said, as the boundaries between our work and home lives become ever more blurred, these ideas have become generalizable to our lives at home as well.

stress, as well as the severity of the stress. Giving a three-hour lecture in front of 250 judgmental strangers will elicit a stronger stress response than watching some over-the-top cable news show for thirty minutes. Either way, cortisol mobilizes our bodies to confront a perceived threat. In this way, stress isn't just a mental challenge we face—it happens inside our body, on a chemical level.

A few months into my journey to calm, while conducting more research into stress and anxiety, I spat into a plastic test tube for a period of a few weeks in the name of understanding my burnout situation. After taking a comprehensive burnout test—the Maslach Burnout Inventory—I found that, as expected, I was diagnosable as having burnt out. But at around the same time, I also became curious about what my cortisol levels were up to, and took the saliva cortisol test.

When we experience a significant amount of chronic stress over an extended period of time—say, after being assigned far too many projects at work or, in my case, after constant business travel—our body gets fed up with constantly going through the whole rigmarole of the stress response. Research has found that when we experience chronic stress for too long, our body "responds by eventually downshifting cortisol production to abnormally low levels." Researchers describe that it's as though "our body's stress response system *itself* has been burned out" (*emphasis mine*).

Usually, our cortisol levels are highest when we wake up in the morning. This is, in part, what mobilizes us to get out of bed. This can also be why we have a tougher time getting out of bed when we're going through an especially stressful period. Our body has downregulated how much cortisol it produces. Figuring that our daily stress will produce it anyway, our body stops its routine cortisol production. Studies suggest that those diagnosed with burnout have far lower cortisol levels in the morning compared with subjects who are not burnt out.[*]

A saliva cortisol test is a less reliable measure of burnout than the Maslach Burnout Inventory (which I'll get to in a second). But I was too curious not to give one a shot. What I found stunned me.

Here's a graph of what our levels *should* look like over a given day, spiking in the morning and falling to more reasonable levels for the rest of the day:

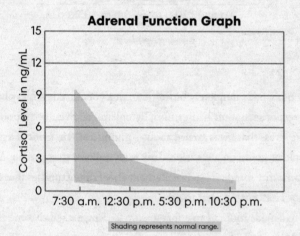

**Adrenal Function Graph**

Shading represents normal range.

Mine couldn't have been more different. When my test results came back, I found that my cortisol levels had essentially flatlined:

---

[*] Interestingly, this is why we can get a bigger boost from caffeine when we consume it at around 10:30 a.m., instead of first thing in the morning. A few hours after we wake up, our cortisol levels are naturally a bit lower, and so too is our energy—in this way, we get a more noticeable energy jolt.

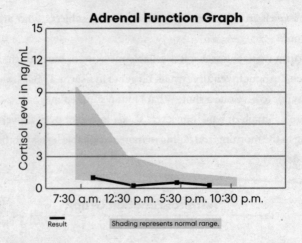

**Adrenal Function Graph**

Result

Shading represents normal range.

My body had completely burnt out. On a chemical level, my body's stress response system had essentially collapsed. Even in response to positive stress that I was *excited* about—giving a talk in front of a group of people or going on a vacation—my body refused to mobilize. At the same time, my mind refused excitement about opportunities that came my way. I had nothing left to give.

If I had made more of an effort to stop feeding myself chronic stress, I would have fared far better.

Instead, I found myself having to climb out of a positive diagnosis of burnout.

## The Burnout Equation

After exploring the research further, I uncovered a few curious ideas about burnout and how it leads us away from calm.

One of these ideas relates to what burnout really is. Feelings of exhaustion are so commonly associated with burnout that people use the two terms interchangeably. But those who make this association miss a full *two thirds* of the burnout equation.

Contrary to common belief, burnout is not just exhaustion. Burnout does leave us feeling exhausted—as well as fatigued, depleted, and worn out. But we also need to feel two other things: *cynical* and *unproductive*. To be fully burnt out, we need all three.

Cynicism is a feeling of detachment in which we feel negative, irritable, withdrawn, and in some cases disassociated from the work we're doing. It's the deeper source of that *take this job and shove it* attitude. With this dimension of burnout, appearances can be deceiving: just because work appears meaningful on the surface doesn't mean it feels that way when we do it. Just ask any healthcare worker who has had to navigate the pandemic. Burnout was a phenomenon initially observed in healthcare—a field that appears to be meaningful on the surface, but that, when you look at the day-to-day activity, is full of sources of chronic stress. (The field, of course, is also chock-full of more meaningful sources of acute stress.)

On top of feeling cynical, we also need to feel unproductive—as if we're not good at what we do or we're not accomplishing enough, like our efforts serve to benefit no one. This dimension of burnout has the potential to fuel a downward spiral: the more burnt out we feel, the more meaningless busywork we engage in. This projects a mirage of productivity to our evaluating mind, but makes us even less productive over time, especially as we take on more chronic stress.

We're not officially burnt out without all three ingredients—exhaustion, cynicism, and feeling unproductive.

Given that this is a book about calm, burnout may seem like a diversion, and, as you'd expect, burnout and anxiety are considered separate constructs by researchers. But burnout is worth exploring, if only because the relationship between burnout and anxiety is so strong. One study found that *59 percent* of those diagnosed as burnt out were also diagnosed with an anxiety disorder—possibly because of chronic stress, given research shows that anxiety can be considered a "condition which acts as a protective factor against threatening situations." Another condition that overlaps with burnout is depression, which many of the ideas in the book may help with. In one study, 58 percent of those clinically diagnosed as having burnt out experienced depression or depressive episodes. While the exact relationship among all three phenomena is unclear, they likely share common antecedents, including chronic stress and other biological factors.

Of course, even setting aside a diagnosis of burnout, experiencing just *one* of the three characteristics of burnout is distressing and can serve as a stepping-stone to the full-blown condition. Generally speaking, if you're feeling exhausted, focus on your workload. If you're disengaged, invest in social relationships, and find ways of connecting more deeply with your coworkers if you can. If you're cynical, identify whether you have the resources you need to do your job, and again whether you can double down on relationships at work.

As I reflected on the events of my work and life that led to the crescendo of the onstage panic attack, little memories flickered through my mind like sparks, reminders of just how depleted I had been. Completing simple tasks felt like moving a mountain. This is a lesson I'd constantly relearn in my journey to calm: that the most simple moments where something didn't feel quite right were the experiences I had the most to learn from. The struggles to get even the most basic tasks done; the times I'd repeatedly reread an email before considering how to respond; the times I could feel my heart sink on a Sunday evening, dreading having to work the following morning.

In another such memory, I recall trying to get some work done on a plane. Responding to emails with my laptop open in front of me, I found myself staring at the same few unimportant emails in my inbox for most of that two-hour flight. Responding to these messages required only a few words and not much thought—but at the time, the task felt like the biggest chore in the world. My mind had thrown in the towel, and I couldn't mobilize to take on the challenge.

Sitting on the plane, I also felt the urge to distract myself to escape this frustration—engaging in busyness to feel productive. I probably should have just closed my laptop and fetched a novel from the overhead compartment. Instead, I engaged with the same pointless few tasks over and over again. I'd wait for emails to come in—and then quickly delete them to reconnect with the mirage of productivity. Refreshing my social media feeds one more time on the laptop, I'd again convince myself I was doing something useful. These distractions fueled the cycle of chronic stress that led me to feel exhausted, unproductive, and cynical.

When I was on a deadline and needed to get stuff done, I was still pretty good at resisting distraction—I set an intention to do something, tamed distraction, and got to work. Off the clock, though, the trap I continually fell in to was engaging with chronic stress when I didn't need to—especially the sources that provided me with validation, like email.

Even after doing my best to tame all the chronic stress I could, I knew I had more work to do.

That's when I spoke with Christina Maslach.

## The Canary

Christina Maslach is a social psychologist and professor emerita at the University of California, Berkeley. She's also the co-inventor, along with Susan Jackson, of the Maslach Burnout Inventory, the single most commonly used instrument for measuring burnout, which has been referenced in scientific literature tens of thousands of times and translated into nearly fifty languages at the time of writing. In doing a deep dive into Maslach's vast body of research, I came across some additional ideas about burnout that put my mind at ease.

The first relates to the ideas of individualism and stress. As I chatted with Maslach, it became clear that one of her greatest frustrations with the popular narrative surrounding burnout is how, much like with the chronic stress we face, we assume that burnout is entirely our fault.

As she put it to me, "So much of how we handle burnout is to weed out the people who 'can't take it,' while telling everyone else to exercise more, meditate, eat healthfully, and take sleeping pills. But what people don't realize is that burnout is not an individual problem to solve—it's a social problem."

As Maslach has written, if we're "finding that [our] workplace is becoming more and more difficult to deal with, then it begs the question of why less attention is being paid to fixing the job" than to fixing *us*.

Unfortunately, in the modern workplace, where there's burnout, there's often also a culture of covering it up. This makes sense: burnout is often perceived as a sign of weakness in workplaces that place high expectations on what employees accomplish with their time—where pretty much everyone is also likely working at capacity. If everyone else can handle the heat, you should be able to, too.

Fortunately for us (and for our mental health), Maslach couldn't disagree more strongly with this notion. "Burnout is viewed as an individual disease, as a medical condition or a flaw or a weakness. The truth is that, even though some of us wear burnout as a badge of honor, it's usually a sign that we're working in an unhealthy workplace that's not a good fit for us." And, if we're experiencing burnout, others likely are, too.

Maslach even goes so far as to identify an occurrence of burnout as a "canary in the coal mine."

The story behind this turn of phrase is a curious one. Canaries take in a large amount of oxygen, and because of this, they can fly at higher altitudes than other birds. Because of their biology, they get a dose of oxygen both when they inhale and exhale. This means that in an underground mine full of toxic gases like carbon monoxide, the birds get a double dose of any poison that's in the air. Sending canaries into coal mines alerted miners to possible dangers before they entered: the canaries were poisoned instead of them. (Poor canaries.)

Maslach considers the canary in the coal mine to be an apt analogy for burnout. In workplaces where she has conducted burnout surveys, she describes the astonishment that those team members experience when they learn that they're not the only person on the team who feels exhausted, cynical, and unproductive.

At one such workplace she surveyed and debriefed, "it was almost a source of pride to work late into the night and not leave until the job was done." When she shared her survey results onstage for this particular team, describing just how many of them admitted to being burnt out, she almost immediately lost control of her audience. People stopped listening: "everyone just started turning around and talking to one another." The moment she gave people a chance to step back, "they realized just how bad the problem was." Had the first case of burnout been more openly discussed and dealt with, perhaps the workplace could have halted its wider descent into toxic levels of overwork and flagging productivity.

In an oddly roundabout way, Maslach herself is quite adept at identifying social environments that have spiraled out of control, including ones others have brushed off as normal. Burnout is, of course, one such phenomenon. Another is one that she encountered early in her career, in 1971—three years before the term "burnout" was even coined by psychologist Herbert Freudenberger. At the time, she was dating a man named Philip Zimbardo (whom she would later marry). He was conducting an experiment at Stanford University that investigated the effects of perceived power and group identity. The experiment designated participants as either "prisoners" or "prison guards," and got them to live out these roles in a mock jail for two weeks.

If you're familiar with the infamous Stanford Prison Experiment, you'll know that it very quickly spiraled out of control. Prison guards turned abusive toward people who had assumed the role of prisoners, who began to think of themselves as *actual* prisoners, not just people in a study. They quickly internalized the stories they had about their role, which became their assumed identity. While the experiment was disastrous, luckily for everyone involved, one person questioned its morality: Christina Maslach. In fact, as Zimbardo, who ran the experiment, would later recount in his book *The Lucifer Effect*, of the fifty people who visited the experiment, Maslach was *the only one* who questioned it and suggested that it be stopped.

She was the canary in the coal mine.

As Maslach would later put it, participants in the experiment had "internalized a set of destructive prison values that distanced them from their own humanitarian values." Compare this with how, in an admittedly far less extreme way, an excessive focus on accomplishment drives us away from thinking about the toll that work takes on our mental and physical health. We feel it's normal to be a prisoner in a job we find chronically stressful. Or, similarly, take how we also quickly adopt new stories around work: work pushes us to assume the role of someone who just has to get through periods of burnout, as if it's some phenomenon we should all experience.

Maslach made clear to me, however, that while burnout might be common, it should not be considered normal. As she refers to it, this "pluralistic ignorance" surrounding burnout is simply not something we should endure or even have patience for.

If you're experiencing burnout—or just feel like you're on your way there—instead of asking what's wrong with you, be more like Christina Maslach, and identify a dangerous working environment if you see one. Being in such an environment can harm your body and mind. As I've mentioned, on a mental level burnout can lead to anxiety and depression at the same time. The physical consequences of burnout quickly pile up, too, as found in one meta-analysis (a study that filters through all prevailing research on a topic and sums up our knowledge about it). This meta-analysis pored over around one thousand studies on burnout and found that it is a significant predictor of too many health factors to mention in one sentence, including "hypercholesterolemia, type 2 diabetes, coronary heart disease, hospitalization due to cardiovascular disorder, musculoskeletal pain, changes in pain experiences, prolonged fatigue, headaches, gastrointestinal issues, respiratory problems, severe injuries and mortality below the age of 45 years." Forget about your mental health—burnout is worth taming for the physical consequences alone.

## The Burnout Threshold

So how can we overcome the phenomenon of burnout?

First, we can reduce how much chronic stress we face. Remember that while burnout has traditionally been defined as a workplace phenomenon, personal stress contributes to burnout, too. The more chronic stress you can tame, the greater the inroads you will make in combating burnout.

The second way we can overcome burnout is by increasing what can be thought of as our "burnout threshold"—how much chronic stress needs to build up in our lives to lead us to burn out. (We'll cover strategies for increasing this threshold in chapter 7.)

Recall that we experience burnout when the chronic stress in our life accumulates to a point where we're no longer able to cope with it

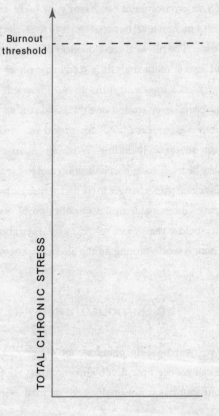

all. In this way, there is a certain burnout threshold we can cross, where the chronic stress of our life is just too much.

With each new challenge, responsibility, or other source of repetitive stress we face—like a significant amount of work travel—we rise a bit closer to this burnout threshold. (We also usually experience more *acute* stress, but chronic stress contributes far more to burnout.) Depending on how much stress we experience across the areas of our life, the layers of chronic stress vary in thickness, as I've illustrated on the

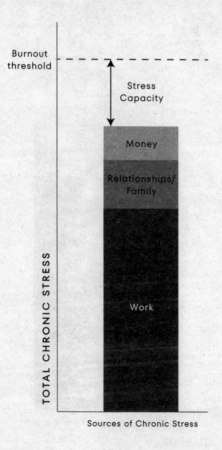

previous page. When we're not burnt out, there's also a healthy gap be-tween how much chronic stress we have and our burnout threshold—this creates a capacity for additional stress, or for us to deal with un-foreseen events that stress us out.

Eventually, though, one too many sources of stress may push us be-yond our capacity. Take the chronic stress that stems from, say, some theoretical global pandemic:

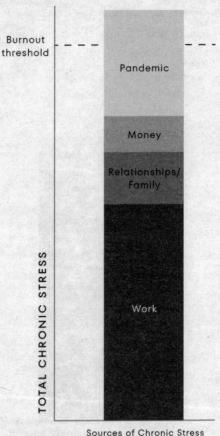

When we start out with a significant amount of chronic stress, a new source of chronic stress must just serve as the straw that breaks the camel's back.

This is yet another reason chronic stress is worth taming: doing so makes us more resilient to *future* stress.

## The Six Burnout Factors

There is a way of understanding burnout even further—a second lesson I'd learn from Maslach. Deconstructing the six factors that contribute to burnout lets us both understand what's causing our situation and gives us the awareness to overcome it.

According to Maslach's research, six areas of our work act as Petri dishes where chronic stress can incubate. The stress that stems from these six areas of our work has been shown, longitudinally over time, to lead us to the burnout threshold—we need just a few of the burnout factors to be out of whack to begin our downward slide. More than one of these factors might be a problem area for you. As you read through this section, pay special attention to how well your job fares in the six areas, and, if you'd like, make a mental note of what your problem areas are. These six factors would apply equally to a full-time stay-at-home parent and the empty nester CEO of a Fortune 500 company.

The first factor of the six is our **workload**—how sustainable the amount of work on our plate is. There is a strong link between our workload and how exhausted we feel (one of the three burnout characteristics). Often, our work demands are too great, and we find ourselves working overtime, during evenings, weekends, and on vacation. The occasional spike in workload is normal—like when we're wrangling a deadline that's threatening to whoosh by—but when every day we face down a workload level that pushes us beyond our usual limits, we never get a chance to recover. Ideally, we have a workload that's roughly equivalent to our capacity to get the work done—this is more likely to lead us to a state of "flow," where we're engaged in what we're doing and time passes by as if it doesn't exist at all.

The second source of burnout is a lack of **control**. This factor is rooted in several issues, including how much autonomy we have, whether we have the resources to deliver work that we're proud of, and whether we have the freedom to shape the projects we're working on. Research shows that the more control we have over our work, the higher our job satisfaction and performance, and the more resilient our mental health. One common source of a lack of control is role conflict—when we have two bosses, or otherwise answer to more than one person or have conflicting demands from multiple people. Researchers have demonstrated a clear and strong link between lack of control and the condition of burnout.

Third, **insufficient reward** dramatically increases our probability of burnout. While we tend to think about money when we think about the rewards of work, money is far from the only currency we derive from our job. Job rewards can be financial (money, bonuses, and stock options), but they can also be social (recognition for the contributions we make), and intrinsic (finding work rewarding in and of itself). The less equitably we're rewarded, the more ineffective we feel—which contributes to the inefficacy dimension that is a core component of burnout.*

---

* If you're a boss, one of the best things you can do for the health of your team is to give more authentic praise to those members doing a genuinely good job. This is simple advice that is worth mentioning for a reason: we don't praise others nearly enough. One study found that, if you're a manager, you can increase the retention rate of new hires to around 96 *percent* with just four instances of praise in a quarter, up from an average of 80 percent. Given the average cost of replacing an employee, each of these four instances of genuine praise could save your team as much as $10,000. As you can imagine, the praise has to be genuine to work—otherwise, it can backfire.

The fourth burnout factor is **community**, which is about the quality of your relationships and interactions at work. We derive an immense amount of engagement and motivation from our working relationships, and experience a great deal of stress in the face of unresolved conflict or a lack of support from colleagues, or when our work environment fosters a lack of trust. An unsupportive work community can be disastrous not only for our productivity, but also for experiencing burnout. It's critical that we feel like we belong.

**Fairness** is the fifth factor. Maslach defines fairness as "the extent to which decisions at work are perceived as being just and people are being treated with respect." A fair workplace promotes employees in an equitable and understandable way, and treats employees with support and respect. Fair workplaces promote engagement instead of burnout. A lack of fairness heavily contributes to the burnout characteristic of cynicism.

The sixth and final burnout factor stems from conflict with our **values**. Essentially, values are what let us connect with our work on a deeper level. When our work connects with what we value, we feel as though we can manifest our values through action, which makes work feel more meaningful. Ideally, our job should provide us with a sense of purpose. If you were initially attracted to your job or career by something other than money, you likely saw how the work aligned with what you actually care about. The less aligned our values are with our team and employer, the less likely we are to find our work meaningful, and the more likely we are to burn out. Research suggests that our values are the key "motivating connection" between us and our workplace. This is about far more than believing in your company's fluffy mission statement: it's about whether you feel as though your work actually matters.

These six factors are so deeply embedded within our work, and in some cases our life, that if you're experiencing burnout, you may need to completely change the work you do (or the team you work with) to no longer experience it. If you're in an environment that stresses you out on most of the six factors, the solution to burnout could be severe, or perhaps improbable: leave, and find a job that actually respects you and your talent.*

Most of these factors are universal—if you're experiencing them, your colleagues likely are, too. If you're up to your neck in stuff to do (workload), with little say over what's on your plate (control), while feeling disconnected from those with whom you work (community), your colleagues probably feel the same way.

That said, some factors, like values, are more personal: what you value is likely to differ from what your colleagues value. For example, if you appreciate community and kindness, and find yourself in a cut-throat, competitive environment, you'll likely become exhausted and disassociate from the work you do. In this way, burnout can signify that your working environment is dangerous for your mental health and well-being, or that your job is just not a good match for your personality and values. (If you want to dig deeper into whether your working environment is toxic or just a bad match, try to find a mentor or colleague you can confide in to pinpoint whether burnout is a widespread problem. If such a person doesn't exist, consider how many of your

---

* If you're a manager who has had one or more employees burn out, you may need to confront an uncomfortable truth: that the working environment you have created for your team is toxic, and your team is facing an unhealthy level of chronic stress. Think deeply about where work is falling short for those on your team by methodically going through the six burnout factors: these are the levers you can apply pressure to in order to increase how happy and healthy your employees are. This will make your team more productive, too, but it goes without saying that their mental health is far more important. (Pay particular attention to the workload, control, and values—research suggests that these are the best levers to start with.)

sources of stress would be faced by someone who is a better fit for your job than you are.) On some level, it really doesn't matter why your job isn't a good fit for you. If you find that you're burnt out or that you're moving in that direction, you need to find a way to mold your work so that it doesn't deplete you. You can do this by determining which of the six factors are out of whack. This lets you see which areas you're struggling in, and make a plan either to improve the situation or to stick things out while actively trying to find a better opportunity somewhere else.

To start:

- Rank, out of ten, how much stress you face from each dimension: workload, control, reward, community, fairness, and values.
- Identify which of the structural problems you're facing in the six areas are fixable—and which ones indicate a toxic work environment that you need to get the heck out of.
- If you still face quite a bit of chronic stress overall, reflect on how strong a fit your job is for you.

Sometimes we have no choice but to work where we do—there are bills to pay, and other companies in our industry may treat employees just as poorly. But there are also windows of time that come along when we can escape a terrible situation, assuming other companies aren't just as bad.

Other times, it's worth working within our company to make things better not just for ourselves but also for the rest of our team. If you're contemplating leaving anyway, this might be worth a shot—if Maslach's research is any indication, other people might feel the same way you do.

If the path to productivity runs straight through calm, a job that leaves you constantly burnt out is a dead end.

## Fixing the Six

In my own journey, I quickly realized that my work was a mixed bag for burnout: I was healthy in some dimensions and unhealthy in others. You're probably in this same boat.

One problem was obvious: I had too much work on my plate, largely in the form of consulting work I had taken on. If you think you're on your way to burnout and think workload is an issue for you, you must do what you can to cut back on your workload level. This is one of the most common clinical interventions that medical professionals recommend for overcoming burnout. Remember: the best way to cut back on chronic work stress is to not experience it in the first place.

One helpful tactic for this is to list all of the activities you do in your work over a month and pick the three that allow you to contribute the most to your team. (You can choose only three.) These are the tasks that you get paid the big bucks (hopefully) to do, or at the very least they're the core of your work. The activities that remain likely support your work, and as a result many of these can be eliminated, delegated, or shrunk so that you spend less time on them, if you have the latitude to do so. If you're burnt out, consider running through this activity with your boss to clarify what's truly most important. Try ranking the tasks that remain by how much stress they cause you. Shrink, delegate, or eliminate the worst offending tasks if possible.

As a stopgap measure, if you can, find little pockets of time throughout the day in which you can remind yourself that you have some time to spare—like by defining some free time within your productivity hours. This creates some breathing room around your work, regardless of how high your workload level is. Set an email autoresponder if you need to: if people need you, they can call. As we covered in the last chapter, setting aside time daily to not think about productivity makes you more productive in the long run.

On top of workload issues, as someone who does mostly solo work, I didn't have much in the way of an immediate community of colleagues to speak of, and, with my consulting work, I felt as though I had almost no control over what projects I took on. (What matters with the six burnout factors is how well we *perceive* we're doing. For example, I had more control over my work than I admitted to myself, but felt as though I didn't. With the phenomenon of burnout, perception matters more than the reality of our situation.)

Luckily, because I run my own business, I could make a plan to improve my situation. After breaking down how my work contributed to my burnout, I stopped consulting for all but the most exciting opportunities—the ones I found the most interesting. I allowed myself to say no without feeling guilty. This led me to earn less money, but crucially, it has let me cut back on chronic stress from travel. While making these changes, I also stopped working with all but a few of my executive coaching clients—the ones I could help the most and grow with together. This allowed me to double down on writing, researching, and training, all of which I find more rewarding, because they help more people (or at least that's the goal). Together, this has lightened my workload and helped me do more meaningful work.

To find more of a sense of community, I also teamed up with a group of other entrepreneurs who do solo work to connect with them every week and hold each other accountable for our goals. As more of us are working from home these days, developing a sense of community with peers is even more critical.

In addition to lowering my workload, these changes increased my perceived level of control, and made the work more rewarding, while letting me connect with a community. I had more capacity for and energy to take on challenges. I'd still have to tame some chronic stress that remained, but at least I was able to take further steps toward calm, while creating space between me and my burnout threshold.

Most of us are a mixed bag regarding how well we're doing across the six areas. If you're feeling some combination of exhausted, cynical, and unproductive, you're probably not struggling with every burnout factor. A single parent in an executive role at a nonprofit may find themselves uniquely struggling with workload and control, but find their days rich in value, community, fairness, and reward. An overbusy single stock trader who works a job strictly for the money may find themselves with a lot of reward and control, but also buried under an immense workload, devoid of things they value, and find it difficult to establish a community with others.

Remember: as with chronic stress and anxiety, burnout does not discriminate based on how much money you make or whether your work makes a difference. All that matters are the six factors.

We'll never be perfect. Chronic stress is harmful, but it's normal to experience some at work; hopefully an amount that's possible to sop up with the stress-relief strategies we'll cover in chapter 7. It's also normal to experience periods during which chronic stress spikes: during a transition at your company, while hunkered down on a new project, or when navigating an endless procession of video calls during a global pandemic.

This is okay. We all go through stress-filled busy periods. Just remember: when most of your chronic work stress is unpreventable and there's no end in sight to the stress you face, that's a situation you need to get out of, or change, however you possibly can. The last thing you need is for your stress response to flatline.

Consider scheduling a recurring event in your calendar to check up on how well you're doing on each of the burnout factors—after going through burnout, I've scheduled a recurring meeting with myself for every six months. Use any time you feel negative, exhausted, or unproductive as a cue to check up sooner.

You may even want to track these variables over time so you can make sure your trend lines are headed in the right direction.

Given how each of these six areas serves as a breeding ground for chronic stress, this activity can prove borderline essential for finding calm.

## CHAPTER FOUR

## The Mindset of More

When the chess game is over, the king and
the pawn go back in the same box.

ANONYMOUS

So far in this book, I've done my best to illustrate how much of a trap the accomplishment mindset is when we do not give it boundaries. Without limits, the mindset leads us to less joy, more busyness, more chronic stress, and a higher probability of burnout, all of which lead us further away from calm. The accomplishment mindset is not the only cause of these factors, of course, but it pours fuel on the fire.

In observing just how commonplace chronic stress, burnout, and anxiety are, I started to dig deeper: If the accomplishment mindset tends to drive so much of what we do, *what leads us to develop an accomplishment mindset?*

The deeper source of the accomplishment mindset is our relentless pursuit of *more*. I define the mindset of more as *a set of attitudes that drive us to strive for more at all costs, regardless of the context*. The accomplishment mindset is just one way that this "mindset of more" manifests.

When we take the mindset too far, "more" becomes the default yard-stick we measure our days against. Did we make more money? Gain more followers? Become more productive? Although our constant striving for more has built the modern world as we know it, we never stop to think: Is *more* the correct variable to optimize our lives around?

For evidence of how pervasive the mindset is, consider how frequently we strive for more of things that *conflict* with one another, in some weird kind of mental jujitsu doublethink:

- We want to become fitter and develop six-pack abs, but we also want to order more Chinese food through our favorite food delivery app.
- We want more quality possessions to fit inside our bigger home, but we also want to have more money saved for a lavish retirement.
- We want more free time, but we also want more productivity and success at work.
- We want more happiness and a more meaningful life, but we also want to cram as much into each moment as possible.

The problem becomes obvious as soon as you see it: "more" is often a delusion. With a constant pursuit of more, we imagine we can always become more affluent, more famous, or more physically fit. (Someone should probably tell Dwayne "The Rock" Johnson this.) We can always find a bigger house, own slightly newer and less-scratched-up gadgets, or sell one more bottle of maple syrup at our novelty souvenir shop. But in reality, useful goals have an endpoint: a point at which a genuine difference is made in our lives. Goals without endpoints are just fantasies.

Again, I'm not advocating that you give up your worldly possessions, or abandon your pursuit of accomplishment if it's something you truly value. It's often worth striving for more—and you shouldn't settle.

However, it is worth reflecting on whether the modern world's default priorities are the right ones for you. If you decide they are, at least you'll have made that decision for yourself. You may decide that just a few things are worth striving for—like love, financial freedom, and leisure time. (Above all else, this is what drives me to productivity: I'm lazy and want more time for what I enjoy.)

We need to question these default goals, taking the ones that fit with our values, while leaving the rest. If you do decide some elements of your life are worth striving for more of, make a plan, and make sure that plan includes an endpoint.

Either way, it's worth reflecting on what drives our behavior. This is especially true when the forces that drive us are hidden, so buried within the world around us that they cannot be seen.

## Costs of More

Taking pains to avoid the mindset of more may sound like a diversion from our pursuit of calm, but it's an essential part of getting ourselves to a less-anxious place. This is true for two reasons: at once, our pursuit of more leads us to more chronic stress, while leading us to structure our lives around the neurotransmitter dopamine, which, as we'll get to shortly, deactivates the calm network in our brain.

Most of us can recognize that boundless striving for more is a hollow pursuit. But what's less obvious is that **more always has a cost**. Often the price we pay is a fine print at the bottom of the ledger of our life's decisions. Taking on a more prominent role at work can drive us to burnout; overeating can make us sluggish and unhealthy; buying a bigger house can lead to more debt, less financial freedom, and more chores. Building a sprawling countryside home may come with an hour-long commute that turns into a long, tedious daily source of stress—while the house requires more maintenance than you have time for. Becoming ultra fit takes a crazy amount of time and energy, which you could be spending on other things, like time with your family or writing a book. (Plus, you probably won't be able to eat as much of what you love.)

Most of these factors differ from person to person, depending on our specific goals and values. But there are some consistencies. For example, research has found that our happiness begins to level off after we earn a household income of around $75,000 (US) a year. This is not to suggest that you should stop striving when you and your partner hit this threshold. But, be mindful of the costs of achieving more past this point—and for this example, adapt this calculation if you live in a city with above- or below-average living costs. Recognize that there will be a point where accumulating more of a given thing no longer serves you.

When *more* is aligned to what we value, and the costs are bearable, striving for it is worthwhile.

More often than we care to admit, the opposite is the case.

Another reason the mindset of more causes chronic stress is that it leads us to buy into the story that *we never have enough*. This is the nagging part of the mindset: no matter how much we accomplish or accumulate, we always feel as though something is *missing*. This constant striving produces perpetual dissatisfaction. Regardless of how much we have, we want more.

This is well illustrated by a study that asked participants how much more money they'd need to be happy. On average, those surveyed said they'd like 50 percent more money than they had already. But here's the thing: this was true *regardless of how much money someone earned.*

Even the multimillionaires wanted 50 percent more! Anecdotally, I know far more wealthy people who are unhappy than people who are low-income earners. This idea maps, curiously, on top of research conducted in the field of savoring, a topic we'll turn to shortly. Savoring is our mind's ability to attend to and appreciate positive experiences. Overall, wealthy individuals report having a diminished ability to savor the positive experiences in their life. One study found that merely being *exposed* to reminders of wealth leads us to enjoy the events of our life significantly less. Instead of becoming present, we focus on what we don't have—while also craving more of it.

Here's a fun scenario to illustrate how the idea of having more money can hijack our happiness. If I offered you a job that paid a whopping $750,000 a year (after tax!), but that job was *guaranteed* to make you permanently and significantly less happy, would you take it?

This shouldn't even be a choice. Yet the mindset of more may lead you to consider the question anyway.

The mindset of more doesn't care how much money you have or how much you've accomplished. It only cares that you strive for more of it all—even if doing so leads you to anxiety and compromises your mental health.

Here's another question to reflect on: How much less money would you spend if, overnight, you stopped trying to impress other people?

Status drives consumption—this was something I found firsthand in my life as I reflected on how I was striving for more. Though this was tough to admit, to myself and to others, there came the point when I began to buy things to show off, rather than because I needed them, or because they made my life better in a tangible way. *More* always made me feel superior—which cost me financially, leading to more chronic financial stress over the years. Chasing status, we're never quite able to enjoy what we have.

My phone was a good illustration of this. I've always been a pretty big tech nerd, and have followed the industry to see how companies push the boundaries of what's possible. But, at a certain point, I began to equate status with owning the latest technology, while judging people by whether they had the latest and greatest. Every year, I'd see my devices as less valuable the moment the new ones came out—even though the device in my pocket didn't change in the slightest. Realizing how much I was judging people based on something so ridiculous made me feel gross. But like it or not, this example is part of a broader idea. We all judge each other on criteria that do not matter, like how much status we project through our material possessions. Just think about how quickly we notice what other people are wearing, or, when meeting someone new, want to place their status relative to ours. (So, what do you do for a living?)

This feeling of superiority provides our brain with a serotonin boost, a neurochemical that provides us with a jolt of happiness. But constantly comparing ourselves with others also leads to more chronic stress—we feel as though we don't measure up.

*More* often does not make a tangible difference. It likely doesn't matter that your phone has three cameras instead of two, that your house has two fireplaces instead of one, or that your couch has some fridge built into it. Personally, I told myself that I appreciated quality items, but I really just wanted to obtain *more* by buying fancier things. (Though I would like to state, in the most emphatic way possible, that I never have and never will own a couch with a built-in fridge.)

A part of this drive to compare ourselves with others is innate. As social psychologist Leon Festinger, the founder of social comparison theory, posited, we have an innate desire to understand how we measure up to others. The mindset of more accelerates this. By activating our comparing mind, the mindset of more leads us to value what's extrinsic (external to us) over what's intrinsic (inside of us). Modern culture tends to value things like money, status, and recognition more than qualities like kindness, helpfulness, and connection—even though these qualities lead to success, too.

While we may *look* successful when we build up what's extrinsic to us—possessions, achievement, and a bigger life—we *feel* successful when we develop what's intrinsic to us—including how calm we are and how much we can actually enjoy our life. At the end of the day, nobody really cares that you live in a big house or that you're a partner at some company. Focusing on the intrinsic leads to far less chronic stress, making us less susceptible to burnout. As author Seth Godin has written, "If you are using outcomes that are outside of your control as fuel for your work, it's inevitable that you will burn out. Because it's not fuel you can replenish, and it's not fuel that burns without a residue."

To paraphrase Maya Angelou, people really won't care how much you accomplish or whether you had more than they do. They'll just care how you made them feel.

## The Chemical of Dissatisfaction

The costs of the mindset of more are substantial—and so are the costs of the accomplishment mindset that the mindset of more spawns. But constantly striving for more is also indicative of a facet of human biology far more profound than either of these states of mind: that our days revolve around the neurotransmitter dopamine. This overabundance of dopamine compromises how calm we feel, heightens our anxiety, and, ironically, can make us less productive in the long run.

Dopamine is a neurochemical that gets a bad rap, but it also has quite a few misconceptions associated with it. It's often called a "pleasure chemical," but this isn't entirely accurate. Dopamine is *associated* with pleasurable things, because our brain bathes itself with the chemical—which induces a thrill-like sensation—whenever we engage in something that has been evolutionarily rewarding to us. That includes finding a mate, eating sweet foods, and accumulating more possessions. But research suggests that dopamine is far more of a chemical of *anticipation* than it is a chemical of pleasure. It is what drives us to behave in ways we think will make us happy. Dopamine does not itself lead to happiness.

Research shows that our brain rewards us with dopamine *immediately before* we engage in something pleasurable—when it's sure that pleasure is on the way. In this way, our brain learns to associate the stimulating behaviors we engage in with a dopamine rush. A dopamine rush feels kind of like a voice, deep down inside of you, is screaming, "Hell yeah!" as you engage in a stimulating thing. This rush reinforces habits that are dopaminergic.

Sometimes the voice of dopamine is faint—like when you check email one more time, or refresh the news once again. Other times it's more pronounced, like when Taylor Swift comments on your Instagram post. But it's usually there, deep down, begging us to engage in what has historically aided our chances at survival.

Dopamine provides the neurological underpinnings of the mindset of more. As Daniel Lieberman, the coauthor of *The Molecule of More* whom I spoke with while I was writing this chapter, put it, "Dopamine has a very specific job: maximizing resources that will be available to us in the future." On top of this, the chemical "cultivates perpetual dissatisfaction." Recall the millionaire who constantly wants to become

50 percent richer. When we are fueled by dopamine, the more we accomplish, the more we strive for more.

In this way, the dopamine that propels the mindset of more creates yet another cycle—this one a cycle of dissatisfaction.

Research suggests dopamine leads us to crave two things that compromise calm: more accomplishment and more stimulation.

I've spent the better part of the last few chapters talking about accomplishment. The more often we strive for greater accomplishment, the more our behavior is driven by dopamine. This is especially true when we don't compartmentalize our dopamine-driven actions through a tactic like productivity hours or a stimulation fast (chapter 6). While every accomplishment has associated costs, I should mention that there is obviously nothing inherently wrong with having aspiration in general. Goals are good, and when we channel our drive directly into the goals that mean the most to us, we can live a better life, one truer to who we are and what we value. But there comes a point at which ambition becomes *generalized*—where we strive for more regardless of the context, and are driven to constantly obtain more extrinsic success. Ceaseless ambition compromises calm.

Ambition is another fascinating and curiously misunderstood phenomenon. Researchers Timothy Judge and John Kammeyer-Mueller define ambition as "the persistent and generalized striving for success, attainment, and accomplishment." It's not necessarily a bad thing: success is fantastic when we use it to serve those around us, including our family and community. And just because we strive for more success does not mean that we strive for more in every area of our life—it's possible to set goals, and strive to achieve them, without those goals taking over your life. (Interestingly, the more conscientious, extraverted, and emotionally stable we are, the more ambitious we tend to be. Ambition is also predicted by one other background variable: the occupational prestige of our parents.)

However, as you might imagine, the *source* of your ambition matters tremendously. Yet another construct that is related to the mindset of more is *greed*, a dispositional trait that represents the mindset of more. As defined by another team of researchers, greed is the "tendency to always want more and never being satisfied with what one currently has." This negatively affects our well-being, because we're never truly able to appreciate what we have or what we've accomplished. Instead of finding a calm state of satisfaction, we move on to the next thing we try to accomplish.

If you happen to be an ambitious person, do remember that constant striving will lead you further away from calm. Ceaseless ambition is often a result of an overreliance on dopamine. With our mind drenched in dopamine, we don't even question why we're striving for more, or why we so rarely savor the fruits of our accomplishments. Blinded by more's allure, we may also forget to consider our values in the decisions we make, or in how we spend our time. We get yet another neurochemical hit whenever we make progress, accomplishing or obtaining something new. In the moment, this feels pretty damn great. So we aim for more still, delaying the opportunity to enjoy a moment of mental calm and savor the fruits of our success.

On top of leading us to crave evermore accomplishment, dopamine leads us to seek out more *stimulation*. Our brain provides us with a satisfying spritz of the chemical each time we pay attention to something novel—social media, email, and the news included. This is what makes taming the sources of chronic stress that we identified in chapter 2 so essential, yet so hard. There's a reason we can't just *choose* to not be distracted, to not go down a multi-hour-long internet rabbit hole. We grow comfortable with some sources of chronic stress, but when stress is dopaminergic, it's addictive.

We want our life's work to have made a difference in the world, but in the moment, we just want to check social media. Every New Year's we set fitness resolutions to achieve throughout the year, but in the moment, we impulsively order takeout and drink a few glasses of wine. Each week, we set work goals that we want to achieve, but at any given moment in the middle of a Tuesday afternoon, we want to keep checking email in order to keep our mind stimulated.

Dopamine takes over.

It's often a bit funny how much we try to cram in to each moment to keep the hits coming. It's no longer enough to just clean the house—we need to listen to a podcast simultaneously to work through our queue. It isn't enough to listen to our favorite piece of music—we also have to simultaneously tend to the busyness layer on our phone. It isn't enough to go for a walk to the grocery store—we need to also listen to an audiobook or talk to a friend. These combinations aren't inherently wrong. But when we combine activities without intention, out of a need for *more*, we do ourselves more harm than good. Busyness can make us feel productive: when our mind is busy, it's also flush with dopamine, which tells our brain that we're productive. But this succumbing to stimulation compromises calm.

We tell ourselves a story about making the most of our time, when we're really just giving in to the neurotransmitter. We naturally want to find what feels good, and provide for ourselves and others, as our evolution has programmed us to do.

And much like with chronic stress and burnout, while this anxious state of chasing stimulation isn't entirely our fault—this is the direction the world pushes us in and how we are biologically hardwired to an extent—it is our responsibility to clean it up.

## A Better Balance

Here's yet another reflection question for you that I found uncomfortable to answer at first: If you were to subtract all of the dopamine-motivated habits, rituals, and actions from your life—all of the websites and apps you compulsively check, and all of what you strive for more of—how much of your day would be left?

Personally, working through this little thought experiment, I wasn't left with much. Much of my striving was aligned with what I valued, sure. But just as much of it involved mindless mental stimulation or seeking more of what I didn't value, including status and material possessions I wouldn't end up using.

For me, this movement from calm began when I first welcomed a smartphone into my life. I loved the thing. With a front that was all screen and a black glossy back that scratched far too easily, this iPhone 3GS was a thing of wonder, let me tell you. It was blistering fast, came with a whopping six gigabytes of monthly data (which, by North American standards, is still sadly a reasonable amount), and let me connect with anyone, anywhere, anytime.

Back then, using it felt like magic. But over time, the device—and not to mention the succession of phones that followed it—only served to compromise my mental health and sense of calm. The device went from being a tool that let me connect with the world to a means to squeeze dopamine hits out of my already burnt-out mind. The more time I spent using the thing, the more often I traded in precious attention for mind-numbing stimulation, while telling myself the story that I was being productive. For me, this is how I first got hooked on dopamine.

Reflecting on this question, maybe as you did, I also unearthed a lot of other stories I told myself while engaging in dopaminergic behaviors. Grabbing at my phone immediately after waking up, still half-asleep, I'd check for new email, telling myself that I had important things to do, not that I needed another spritz of the neurochemical. Flipping through my social media feeds over breakfast, I'd tell myself that I was taking a break before a hectic day, not that I was again seeking ever more stimulation. On a work break or bored during a Zoom call, I'd get another hit by checking the news in a different window, telling myself that I needed to be informed of everything going on in the world. *I'm not getting anything done anyway*, my self-talk fired.

Unfortunately for us living in the modern world, dopamine-driven habits fill the little in-between gaps of our days like water, drowning out any opportunity for genuine reflection, rest, or calm.

Once again, don't beat yourself up over this! A large number of your habits may be propelled by this neurochemical, and in many cases, that's okay. Thankfully, it's possible to reclaim balance by eliminating *unnecessary* dopamine-driven habits.

What does balance look like in practice? Or better yet, what does it *feel* like?

If you think your attention span used to be longer than it is now, you're not wrong, and you're not alone. Before a modern world pushed us to center our lives on stimulation and accomplishment, we could feel calm and present with relative ease. We could leave the office and, when we got home, fall into a good book on the couch for an hour or two. We didn't divide our attention across a couple of screens simultaneously.

Starting our day off slow, after hitting snooze a time too many on the newfangled digital alarm clock plugged into the wall, we calmly thought about the day that lay ahead, or just what we should have for breakfast. We turned inward to plan our day, not immediately outward to seek stimulation. If you've ever watched an older movie and felt calmed by the absence of devices, you need not worry. It's possible to find this same balance again while still getting what you want out of technology.

Fortunately for us, much as there are dopamine-fueled networks in our brain associated with stimulation and accomplishment, *there are networks we can activate in order to find calm*. Interestingly, the brain networks for both dopamine and calm are even *anticorrelated* with each other: when our dopamine network is activated, the calm network isn't, and vice versa.

Neuroscientists like Lieberman refer to the calm network inside our brain as the "here-and-now" network: it's what lets us enjoy ourselves and allows us to feel a satisfying presence with what we're doing. It's the mode you enter into as you savor your morning cup of coffee at the cottage, the mode that's activated as you become mesmerized by the campfire at night. If the dopamine network is all about maximizing our future, the here-and-now network reminds us that our work is done; that it's time to slow down, rest, and savor what the present has to offer. The here-and-now network lets us show up in our own lives, become deeply immersed in the moment, and, above all, stay present with who and what are in front of us.

By reducing our dependence on dopamine, we find a better balance. We alternate between the dopamine and calm networks more effortlessly, just as we could before dopamine took over our lives, when we were the free spirit who did things for the sake of doing them.

• • •

While dopamine rushes are a thrill, the here-and-now network in our brain has neurochemicals associated with it that are just as powerful, not to mention wonderful. The main neurochemicals that are associated with this calm network are **serotonin** (which makes us feel happy), **oxytocin** (which makes us feel connected), and **endorphins** (which make us feel a sense of euphoria).* Dopamine is associated with our brain's calm network, too, though in less concentrated amounts, usually balanced with these other chemicals simultaneously. If you've found that most of your day revolves around dopamine, you may be in need of these chemicals.

I'll explore the role of these neurotransmitters in depth later on. For now, I'll just say that if you feel less satisfied and connected to others than you did years ago—perhaps before getting your first smartphone, or before your working environment turned into a hyperconnected one—you're not alone. Engaging in any dopaminergic habit suppresses activity in the brain's calm network. In turn, this suppresses signals that we should stop working and instead enjoy what we've accomplished.

Much like the productivity spectrum, balance here is critical: we don't want to be overinvested in either network! Much as a dopamine-centered life can lead to, as Lieberman calls it, a "productive misery," an overinvestment in the here-and-now network can lead to an overabundance of laziness.

It's important that we strike a balance between striving and savoring.

Luckily for us, there are ways of doing so—and we'll get to the first

---

* It's worth noting that these descriptions are generalizations—the effects of these neurotransmitters are complex and tough to reduce to one sentence. Overall, though, these are the effects they produce.

of them now. As it turns out, there is a crucial ingredient we can invest in to combat our overreliance on dopamine—one that, curiously, serves to both energize us and help us overcome burnout at the same time.

## Driven by Purpose

If you can't tell, I'm a fan of reflection questions. Here's another prompt for you to consider: *What is the exact opposite of burnout?*

Have an answer in mind?

In addition to leading us to become less present, a dopamine-centered life can also, quite ironically, lead us to become less productive.

Driven by dopamine, we waste more time on distraction, while shortening our attention span through constant stimulation. We also lose control of our behavior more often, especially online—acting on autopilot mode in response to whatever stimuli happen to be in front of us instead of intentionally setting a course for ourselves. These factors make us less productive. But there's another factor that makes us less productive still: a dopamine-centered life can lead us to become *less engaged with our work*.

Yet another fascinating discovery that Christina Maslach has made through her burnout research is that **the polar opposite of burnout is *engagement***. In fact, by flipping the three characteristics of burnout around (through the ideas in the previous chapter), we *convert* burnout into engagement. When we're burnt out, we're exhausted, unproductive, and cynical. When we're engaged, we feel energized, productive, and driven by purpose.

Even if you're *not* burnt out, reversing the factors that lead to burnout is the process through which you can become more engaged at work and in every facet of your life.

If you've invested time in the tactics I've shared so far, that effort is about to pay dividends. We've already laid much of the groundwork for engagement. Chronic stress leads us to burnout, and so by taming sources of it in our life, we become less burnt out and more engaged *simultaneously*. This also applies to the chronic stress we pay attention to by choice. Taming these distractions reduces activation in our brain's dopamine circuits, while increasing activity in our brain's here-and-now network. In this way, reducing chronic stress leads us to calm, while making us more engaged, focused, and present. It'll make us more productive to boot: not a bad payoff, even once you account for how tricky some sources of stress are to tame.

As I tamed more of my own sources of chronic stress, and dealt with the six burnout factors, I found myself becoming more engaged with what was in front of me, without any additional interventions on my part. I've written about the power of taming distraction in my previous books—this lets us get out of our own way and makes focus effortless. Taming chronic stress—especially its hidden sources—allowed me to elevate my focus to a new height. I could just ease into working on whatever was in front of me. I still faced resistance, as we all do, but that decreased to a fraction of what it had been before. (I still craved dopaminergic distractions because of their stimulating properties, but we'll cover this idea in the chapters to come.)

For now, though, just remember one thing: when you tame enough chronic stress, engagement comes naturally. And with engagement comes calm.

This is far easier said than done. But given that engagement leads us to both greater productivity *and* calm—while leading us to worry less about whether we have enough—reconnecting with it is a worthwhile endeavor.

## Tracking Engagement

Over time, I'd discover what a superpower engagement can be. Engagement is the process through which we actually become more productive at work and intentional in our lives—and this is especially the case when we're engaged with our most consequential tasks, the ones through which we make the biggest difference. Ultimately, it's engagement that makes us productive in the long run: when we're engaged, we actually work toward our goals. Engaged, we eschew dopamine-riddled distraction, because it doesn't contribute to what we're doing. Remaining present, rather than stimulated, we move our work and life forward.

We also *feel* like we're accomplishing more when we're engaged with what's in front of us. Instead of setting goals that we continually push just beyond our reach while craving more, when we're engaged, we're focused, deliberate, and fired up about what we're doing. We enjoy the process of what we're doing far more—while concurrently working to, over time, strike a more reasonable balance between striving and savoring, and rebalance our mind for calm.

So how can we put this into practice?

The first step is laying the groundwork I've covered so far in the book. There is no better way to become more engaged than eliminating unnecessary chronic stress, especially the stress contained within the six burnout factors. As I hope you'll find, the return on your time and effort in taming sources of chronic stress will prove remarkable—

and might just be the fuel you need to tame those sources of stress for good.

After you've laid this groundwork, here are a few more ideas for reconnecting with engagement, all of which worked for me in my journey to calm:

- **At the end of each workday, reflect on how engaged you were.** There is no right or wrong way to measure your days or your life—your values and circumstances should inform the benchmark you use. But for me, more than any other factor, engagement is the variable I've started reflecting on most after poring through the research on calm. Over time, it has become how I personally measure my workdays, along with how well I performed during my productivity hours. I've come to think of engagement as the metric we should optimize our workdays around. At the end of each day, ask yourself: How immersed was I in my work today? How often did I give in to dopamine to stimulate my mind with busyness—and how often was I able to be present with what I was doing? On top of this, it's helpful to reflect on whether what you engaged with was essential and meaningful.

- **Work slower.** The best part about striving for engagement instead of stimulation is that you don't need to work as frantically. As your mind adjusts to fewer dopamine hits, it'll become calmer, and you'll naturally dive deeper into what you're doing. You'll rediscover engagement, instead of seeking *more* for more's sake. There is a great joy to be found in working with a thoughtful deliberateness on what's important. If you value productivity as I do, don't worry: what you'll lose in speed, you'll easily earn back in making progress on what's important. This is a lesson I'm continually relearning when it comes to doing deep knowledge work: the more slowly I work, the more impact my work tends to have. I produce more of what I'm proud of over time.

- **Notice what dopamine-fueled stressors creep back into your life.** Taming hidden sources of chronic stress (and not to mention distraction) is not a one-time endeavor: it's a constant game of whack-a-mole you'll need to engage in in order to protect your mental health. The game becomes easier as you disengage from dopaminergic habits and engage more with the here and now. You'll find that doing this is the opposite of a video game: it starts out hard and ends easy. Look out for distractions that creep back in, and also notice the stories you tell yourself about why you need to engage with them.

- **Maintain an accomplishments list.** As you become less busy, you'll feel less productive—even though you'll likely accomplish just as much (if not more). A terrific counterweight to this mental bias is to keep an accomplishments list. The definition is in the name: as the week goes on, jot down the milestones you hit with your work, the projects you ship, and the progress you make. It's remarkable how much more we can get done when we become more engaged and less busy.

- **Mind your engagement level as you face varying levels of chronic stress over time.** As you deal with the chronic stress that originates in your six burnout factors and the other areas of your life, notice whether you become more engaged at work and have more energy to stay engaged at home. When it comes to making changes to your habits, awareness is vital: noticing improvements reinforces the habits you're investing time, attention, and energy into.

- **Set goals with an accomplishment mindset, but work toward them with an eye on engagement.** Begin your productivity hours by considering what you want to use them to accomplish—but then focus on how engaged you are after that point, investing in the tactics above. I think you'll find the same thing that I have: by focusing on engagement—the process through which you become productive—you'll accomplish more during these hours.

Chronic stress deteriorates the shield that protects us from an over-busy, overanxious world. This is often a consequence of going with the flow of dopamine.

When we actively fight against this force, we discover greater depths of calm.

## The Science of Savoring

In addition to noticing how engaged you are as you tame chronic stress, another strategy for overcoming the mindset of more is finding things to savor. Like engagement, this tactic shifts the activation in your brain's dopamine networks to the calming here-and-now network. Over time, this leads you to become more present, especially as you deal with the most problematic dopaminergic superstimuli, the subject of the next chapter.

One of my favorite things to ask someone when I meet them for the first time is this: *What do you savor the most?* In asking dozens of people this question, I have been surprised at how many people just don't have an answer. This is especially the case for men: research shows that women report having "greater savoring capability" and that this gender difference is "found from middle childhood to older adulthood and across culture." This also holds true for the most successful people I know: the question leaves them dumbfounded and speechless, often for several seconds, as they process the question and gather their thoughts. (Recall the study that found that wealthier individuals report a diminished ability to savor life's experiences. As the researchers who conducted this study summed up, "wealth may fail to deliver the happiness one might expect because of its detrimental consequences for savoring.")

We all need an answer to the question of what we savor. Better yet, we need *several* answers.

Before we began constructing our days around dopamine, this question didn't stump most of us as it does now. We savored the downtime we had at a rented cottage in that middle sweet spot of summer; the serendipitous conversations we struck up with the person seated next to us on the plane; the delicious, disorderly dinners we shared with extended family. We savored the time we spent playing board games in the kitchen and word games on long family road trips, and we could certainly slow down enough to enjoy the rich taste of our morning cup of coffee.

Driven by dopamine, we rarely, as Billy Joel sings in "Vienna," "take the phone off the hook and disappear for a while." Rushing past the most beautiful moments of our life—should we notice them at all—we find it oddly challenging to deeply savor things. Propelled forward by the mindset of more and the mindset's dopaminergic underpinnings, this is a tendency we must actively counterbalance.

Savoring provides us with a unique opportunity to deliberately disengage from the accomplishment mindset, to set our ambitions aside, and to actually enjoy ourselves for a while. Again: What's the point of accumulating accomplishments when you don't enjoy the fruits of them along the way? By practicing savoring—and indeed, it is a practice, as well as a science—we disengage from our goals and immerse ourselves in the delightful happenings of the present moment.

Viewed another way, we practice purposeful inefficiency, where we set aside our accomplishment goals, and switch to a mindset of deliberate enjoyment. (Don't worry, your goals will always await you on the other side of savoring something.)

**Here's my challenge for you: make a list of everything you savor.** If you need ideas, look to the quiet moments in your life you used to enjoy a whole lot more, perhaps before you got a smartphone or before there was a pain-in-the-ass pandemic. If you find this a challenge, think about the satisfying moments in your day that you rush past to get stuff done. Capture these items somewhere you can refer back to on a regular basis.

At the start of my calm journey, if I'm honest, savoring felt like a chore. But I captured a list of stuff I could anyway, to try savoring on for size. Some of the things on my list included, in no particular order:

- Any book by Elizabeth Gilbert, Stephen King, Beverly Cleary, or Neal Stephenson
- A walk through the forest near where I live
- A fancy, overpriced macadamia nut milk latte from the café down the street
- My morning matcha ritual
- Walking downtown with my phone on airplane mode, listening to piano instrumental music (also a great soundtrack to work to)
- The feeling of a new type of mechanical keyboard (I highly recommend "Cherry brown" key switches if you're ever in the market for one)

- Sweaty workouts on a spin bike
- Reading the morning newspaper with that aforementioned cup of matcha
- Wine-filled cribbage game nights with my wife

The list goes on, but you get the idea.

**Each day, pick one thing on your list and savor it deeply.** Spend as much time on the list as you want—but spend time on the list every day. When you notice that your mind has run off to think about work or anything else, gently bring it back, refocusing on the pleasant experience you're having.

Also mind the stories you tell yourself about this activity. Reading these words, your self-talk might be going through the roof; your dopamine circuitry may be going haywire, not wanting to do this challenge. Don't worry: you have the time to do this. You may have to steal some time away from the busyness layer. That's okay: just remember that, over time, doing this will help rewire your brain for calm and engagement. You'll get this time back.

One of the great joys of embarking on the journey to calm was researching the scientific underpinnings beneath the tactics I was exploring (and now, sharing). In this process, one of the most delightful fields of research I encountered was the field of savoring. Indeed, research has discovered remarkable benefits to deliberately enjoying life's positive experiences.

On average, we experience around three good things for every bad thing—a ratio that has been replicated time and again in research. Despite this being the case, our threat-finding mind processes negative information more thoroughly than it does positive information. This negative rumination leads directly to anxiety—not to mention an underestimation of how great our life actually is.

This is backward. Situations in life can be challenging—and we all have a different ratio of good-to-bad things. But overall, three to one is the ratio most of us get to work with. If our overall mental state were to match our reality, we would feel calm—not stressed or anxious—around three quarters of the time. Luckily, it's possible for us to "swish more experiences around in our mind," as Fred Bryant, the psychologist who pioneered the research field of savoring, put it to me. We can use lessons from research conducted on savoring to notice the positive experiences in our life, prolong them, and make them more meaningful. In this way, meaning is not something that we find—it's something that we notice, in our lives and in the world around us. This is where savoring fits in.

When we deliberately enjoy the positive experiences that comprise our day, we become happier, calmer, and more engaged—at the same time.

In his research, Bryant contends that the happiest people have one thing in common: they savor positive experiences more deeply. High levels of savoring, as you might expect, lead to greater engagement, as well as less anxiety. The very act of savoring positive experiences prolongs them, and having a greater capacity to savor positive events leads to less depression and social anxiety. Also, the better we become at savoring positive experiences, the less family conflict we experience, the better we feel about ourselves, and the more resilient we become. Higher savoring ability is correlated with higher levels of mindfulness, optimism, and even wisdom. One study found that the act of savoring leads to significantly fewer depressive symptoms—while another found that savoring led older adults to have "maintained higher life satisfaction, regardless of their level of health." These correlations should give you pause—especially considering that savoring, as Bryant says, "is a skill that grows with practice." We may need to prioritize savoring to enjoy the fruits of our productivity daily, but the benefits are profound when we do.

Savoring is the art of enjoying the good things in life, and can be thought of as the practice through which we convert positive *moments* into positive *emotions*—like joy, awe, pride, and pleasure. When savoring, we pay attention to and enjoy the entirety of a positive experience.* According to Bryant, savoring doesn't just let us enjoy our experiences more: it also helps us strike a balance between striving and enjoyment. Per his research, there are four main ways we exert control over our life experiences. With negative experiences, we can either avoid them or cope with them. With positive experiences, we can either focus on obtaining more of them (with what Bryant calls an "acquisition mentality") or savor them.

The very act of savoring lets us set aside the mindset of more so we can enjoy ourselves. As Bryant puts it, "Just because you've obtained something doesn't mean that you'll enjoy it. In fact, you're often just driven onto the next thing you want to acquire." We don't automatically feel grateful, and if we're not careful, we focus far too much on *getting* and not enough on savoring. "That's the trouble with the acquisition mentality: what good is getting something if you don't enjoy it?

---

* There is some conceptual overlap between savoring and the constructs of both flow and mindfulness—two separate yet tangentially related topics. According to Bryant, flow is different because it "implies far less conscious attention to the experience." Flow also implies working on a relatively challenging task that roughly matches our skill level. Savoring is also different from the construct of mindfulness because it's more restrictive: we're only focused on what's positive, instead of observing our experiences with nonjudgmental awareness.

You're never looking at what you do have. You're looking at what you don't have and what you need to get."

The options for how we can savor something are endless. Bryant's research indicates that there are multiple ways we can savor an experience, including by practicing *luxuriating* (basking in the pleasure something creates), *marveling* (feeling awe and wonder about something), and *thanksgiving* (appreciating the good things in your life). Each night, before we fall asleep, my wife and I share three things we're grateful for with each other. Simple gratitude habits like this don't just feel good: they lead you to enjoy life more and to notice more positive events around you—expressing gratitude is yet another way of savoring what you have.

We can even savor a *past* or *future* experience. (This still counts as savoring because we enjoy the feelings in the present moment.) When we savor the past, we practice *reminiscence*, which makes us feel grateful for our past experiences. (We can do this by replaying an enjoyable moment in our head.) Savoring the future can prove slightly more difficult in practice, but when we do, we practice *anticipation*, ramping up our excitement about something that has yet to happen (like by counting down the days to a vacation). Interestingly, the act of anticipation has been shown to lead us to enjoy an experience even more deeply when it eventually does happen—and, later on, look *back* at the experience more fondly. One theory for why this happens suggests that anticipation "creates affective memory traces that are reactivated and integrated into the actual and remembered consumption experience."

Whether you prefer to savor the present, past, or future—through luxuriating, marveling, or thanksgiving—the benefits of doing so are profound.

Savoring isn't just a shortcut to engagement. It's also a shortcut to enjoyment.

• • •

The first time you try savoring on for size, you may find the ritual difficult, and your brain will resist it—your negative self-talk will likely go through the roof. In a world that values more, savoring the moment feels like an act of rebellion. You may even give in to the resistance a time or two—checking Instagram or email, or thinking about all you have to do after.

While this is normal, I challenge you to resist this urge. But do notice it, while bringing your attention back to the nice experience you're having.

Notice all that you can during the ritual. Notice any boredom you experience as your mind comes down from stimulation. Notice what you crave: devices you impulsively want to reach for, ideas you want to jot down, things you automatically start planning for. Notice your self-talk, too. Are you overly hard on yourself because you set aside the accomplishment mindset, not to mention the mindset of more? Are you still thinking about the opportunity cost of your time, or telling yourself that savoring stuff is dumb? Do you feel selfish for investing in your energy, and developing your capacity for presence (the skill of being with what you're doing)? How much guilt do you feel from not working, or moving forward with your goals?

This resistance is normal—expected, even—as you rewire your brain for calm engagement, instead of anxious distraction.

Over time, deploying this tactic and the others I'll share shortly, you'll begin to notice the positive effects of a rebalanced mind. You will not only show up more in your work and life, you'll also develop a capacity for focus as the cloud of dust in your mind settles. You'll deepen your ability to find happiness and connection. And you'll feel energized and refreshed.

You may also find that savoring makes you more grateful for all you have, including the little things. The great irony of the mindset of more—and the accomplishment mindset—is that both are constructed on top of a dopaminergic life, so neither leads to lasting satisfaction.

Unlike these mindsets, savoring leaves us satisfied.

The mindset of more permits us to feel comfortable with ourselves only when we suddenly find ourselves with more than what we expected to have—more money in the bank, more followers, more friends. But these feelings are fleeting and ephemeral. It's possible to feel a sense of abundance far more often.

There is already so much good in our life—we just need to notice it.

Savoring one simple thing a day is a simple tactic. Like any idea in this book, it works alongside the others to lead to calm. But its true magic is how it works to erode the negative aspects of our constantly seeking more: we can set aside striving and remain present with what we're doing. This helps us show up for the rest of our life, too, by leading us to appreciate the here and now—where both calm and productivity live.

Achieving more is great, and you may indeed want to obtain more in your life. But as I hope you find, while the accomplishment mindset may work in some areas of our lives, it's by training our brain to savor that we can set this mindset aside to find balance. We accomplish what we intend to, while actually enjoying life.

In all of these marvelous ways, savoring the present—the here and now—leads us to overcome our constant striving for more and reach greater depths of calm.

## CHAPTER FIVE

## *Heights of Stimulation*

## Personalized Stimulation

To continue our exploration into how the modern world compromises our sense of calm, let's take a short detour to talk about digital distraction. The reason for the detour is important: in the modern world, a great amount of our dopamine comes from the digital world.

Take YouTube, for example. As I write these words, there are billions of videos you could watch on YouTube. The scale of the website is so enormous that writing about its size is surprisingly tricky—there's no figurative quarter you can place next to the site to imagine its scale. Over five hundred *hours* of video are uploaded to the site every *minute*. That's thirty thousand days' worth of new content added every twenty-four hours. Technically speaking, YouTube is the second-largest search engine globally, after only Google, which owns YouTube.* YouTube is also the second-largest website globally, even after you include websites that are predominantly accessed in China—the world's most populous country—like Tmall and Baidu. Localized versions of YouTube are available in more than eighty languages, in more than one hundred

---

* Also technically speaking, the holding company *Alphabet* owns both YouTube and Google, though Google is the umbrella company that runs Alphabet's internet businesses. A similar idea holds true for *Meta,* the holding company that owns Facebook.

countries, and every day videos on the website generate billions more views. And, get this: 2 billion logged-in users—around one quarter of all living humans—visit the website every month. YouTube can also be considered the second-largest social media website, after only Facebook, with around 2.7 billion users.

It's not just videos for "Baby Shark" and "Gangnam Style" generating all this traffic. YouTube is the de facto video hub of the internet. This means that the categories of videos on the site are endless: product reviews, how-tos, vlogs of people living their daily lives, talk show clips, and videos of people playing video games included—a phenomenon I'll probably never understand, no matter how often my younger cousins try to explain it to me. And that's okay: with such a deep catalog of content, not every video will be a good fit for me. I probably won't even like most of them.

I'm not supposed to.

If you squint your eyes a bit, YouTube is what you'd get if you took broadcast television and flipped it on its head. Television is designed to appeal to the masses, while YouTube surfaces content that appeals most uniquely to *you*. Unlike a TV channel, which can broadcast only one show at a time and must dilute content enough so that it appeals to as many people as possible, YouTube can play a different video for every user on the website. There are also no practical limits to how much content can exist on YouTube—Google can always buy up more cheap storage space for its server farms. Five hundred additional hours of new content every minute? No problem.

There's also no limit to how niche content can be. It's *better* if content is niche: when you stumble upon the videos that appeal uniquely to you, you'll enjoy them that much more. Everyone wins, or at least that's the theory: you spend more time on the site, and Google has more time to show you ads. You'll consume more novel content, and Google makes more money.

As I look through my own recommended videos on the site at this very moment, there are videos about the switches used in mechanical computer keyboard keys, science videos about astronomy, and hour-long clips from old Steve Jobs keynote presentations.

You're unlikely to like all these same videos—this unique feed of content is designed to appeal to just me. That's why I keep coming back.

If you use the site, this is why you keep coming back, too.

## A Mountain of Data

Theoretically, amid the enormous sea of videos on YouTube, there is the perfect one for you. There is the one video that will make you laugh so hard that you lose control, cry your eyes out for twenty straight minutes while forever changing how you think about a topic, or inspire you to lose twenty pounds over the next two months and keep them off for the rest of your life. This video is probably on the website, somewhere. YouTube's job is to find it for you.

One of the main core competencies of Google (if not its main one) is designing algorithms. These algorithms serve up everything from web search results to YouTube recommendations to search results in Gmail to routes on Google Maps. One of the company's primary algorithms is obviously web search: for most people, Google's name is synonymous with the activity of searching on the web. We don't Duck Duck Go anything or Bing our way to a website: we google stuff. My computer's spell checker didn't even try to capitalize the company's name in that last sentence: the name has become generic.

If there is indeed a perfect video for you in the sea of billions, how would a product like YouTube find a way to show it to you?

Basically, the same way a human would: by learning as much about you as possible. The more the company knows about what you like, the more tailored your recommendations can be. By capturing information like your interests, personality, mood, and income level—and inputting this data into a sophisticated algorithm—the company can determine the most tempting video for you right now. It's incredible when you think about it, especially given it all happens in a second or two. It's also kind of scary—especially as far as our fractured relationship with dopamine is concerned.

I should say that very little information has been published about the criteria that YouTube's algorithm weighs and takes into account. Recommendation algorithms are a proprietary competitive advantage. But we can at least try to paint a picture of the kind of data Google keeps about us, by looking at what information *we* might crunch to find that perfect video if we were running YouTube; to find the content that's most dopaminergic and likely to keep users coming back for more.

If you're an average user, YouTube already knows a lot about who you are. For starters, it knows your search and watch history, along with which channels you enjoy content from and where you are logging in from (based on your computer's IP address). Even if you're *not* logged in, the site knows videos you hover over to see a preview and what time of the day it is when you visit the site—because you'll watch different videos on your lunch break than during an early morning bout of insomnia.

It's no wonder YouTube nudges us to log in so frequently: this way, when we're logged in, Google can connect our YouTube data with all else that it knows about us. For starters, if you're logged in to your

Google account and search for information online using Google, You-Tube knows what you've searched for on the internet. This alone will be enough to understand you deeply, nail down your interests, and know what your mood is like these days.

If you use the Chrome web browser, especially if you have Chrome's "sync" feature turned on—which syncs your bookmarks and history across devices and keeps you logged in to your Google account—the company could theoretically crunch all of this information about you, too.

If you use Gmail, the company has information about whom you communicate with (your social graph), which newsletters you sub-scribe to, and what you buy online. (Amazon and other companies now hide purchase information in their confirmation emails, potentially so companies like Google can't add this information to your profile.)

If you use Google Maps, the company knows where you travel to, which restaurants you frequent, and which modes of transportation you use. The service may also know what trips you have coming up.

If you're an average internet user and visit sites without an internet ad blocker, the company also knows many of the sites you visit. The company's Analytics product, which monitors your behavior on a site so the website's owner can collect traffic statistics, tracks information about how long you spend on the site, which pages you visit, and how you got to the website in the first place.

The list goes on—you may provide Google with even more infor-mation through your Google Drive account, smart speaker, and Google News. The data Google has on you could fill an entire book. (Don't worry, I'll stop here.)

The basic idea behind all this is simple, though: the more personalized our video recommendations, the more dopaminergic they become—and the more we get hooked and come back for more.

## The Era of Novelty

As the old cliché goes, it is always helpful to "follow the money" in order to understand the motivations of a for-profit business. In the case of YouTube, I've already mentioned the primary thing the app is optimized to accomplish: keeping you on it! Zooming out from this example, you will find this is true for most other services structured on top of an algorithm. The more time you spend on services such as Instagram, Twitter, and YouTube, the more money each service makes. They simply have more time to show you ads in between the content that keeps you hooked. At the time of writing, Google makes a whopping *80 percent* of its revenue from a single source: *advertising*. It has earned this proportion of income for over a decade—a surprisingly stalwart and reliable source of revenue in the turbulent, famously disruptive world of Silicon Valley.

Facebook is the same. Actually, that isn't entirely true: its percentage is far *higher*. In the most recent year at the time of writing, Facebook made *97 percent* of its revenue from advertising. Together, the two companies absorb 61 percent of the advertising money on the internet. If you're ever looking for something fun to do, try poking around the settings in Instagram to discover your "ad interests."* While Instagram may get a few things comically wrong, you'll find that it is oddly adept at finding out who you are. To assemble your list of interests, Instagram monitors activity on your Instagram and Facebook accounts, while, according to the news website Mashable, even siphoning "infor-

---

* I would include instructions on how to do so, but the path to this feature within the app will change either leading up to or after the publication of this book. Just *Duck Duck Go* how to find this feature.

mation from third-party apps and websites you've logged in to through Facebook."

I had disabled Instagram ad tracking before researching this section of the book, but thankfully took screenshots of the interests of mine that Google had identified before disabling the ad personalization "feature" on my account. I found that Google had identified *177 specific interests* of mine. While some of these slightly missed the mark (like nightclubs, combat sports, luxury vehicles, and soccer, none of which are strong interests), nearly all of the items on the list were accurate—even eerily so. That included interests as esoteric as: audio file formats and codecs, clocks, development tools, distributed computing, home automation, Nintendo, proxying and filtering, sound libraries, TV comedies, visual art and design, and yoga.

I quickly disabled ad personalization after seeing the list.

My YouTube recommendations now suck. But at least I now buy less stuff after disabling the same feature on Instagram.

The greater the likelihood that a data company's algorithm can surface the perfect piece of content for us—whatever their equivalent of the perfect YouTube video happens to be—the more we'll stick around and come back for more. It's no surprise, then, that some services, such as Instagram and Twitter, have in recent years moved away from chronologically arranged timelines to personalized ones that present first the morsels of content most likely to hook us.

The content that hooks us also releases quite a bit of dopamine and, as a consequence, drives us away from calm. Because services like Google and Facebook make money through paid advertising, they can then charge companies to put annoying ads in front of our eyeballs. We're hooked enough that we don't mind, and they can optimize their service to show us a number of ads that won't affect how much time we spend in the app. The more time we spend in-app, the more dopamine that gets released in our brain, and the further away we move from calm.

Think about it: in the case of Google, pretty much every service that the company offers, from Google Docs to search to YouTube, is free. Yet the company is worth more than one trillion dollars.

Working with advertisers, that is how much economic value it has been able to extract from us and our data.

Writing about this stuff, I may come across like some paranoid guy who wears tinfoil hats and builds pyramids in his backyard to ward off aliens. I promise I'm not—though I do find that the hats ward off some of those 5G wireless rays. (Kidding.) This much is just a fact: many tech companies make money from our data.

As it relates to calm, I firmly believe that personalization algorithms make it so content platforms—especially social media platforms—are no longer a positive or neutral presence in our lives. Our digital world now actively drives us away from calm, because of how it hooks us with content that releases dopamine.

Particularly in an already anxious world, personalized online content can upheave our neurochemistry. Algorithms don't discriminate based on which videos, images, or updates are good and bad for us. Social networks are not paternalistic either: most of them do not have malicious intent; they're just in the business of making money.

And let's be honest, can you blame them? Companies are not charities. This is especially true for companies hooked on growth, founded in a culture of more. The larger a company grows, the richer its founders and employees become. A data company's surest path to growth is making money off our data. The way it does this is by providing us with more dopamine hits.

On the surface, the fact that our digital world is more engaging might sound like a good thing. Sure, we waste more time tapping on glass screens, jumping between Instagram, TikTok, Reddit, and Twitter. But if we're spending more time on these services, aren't we more entertained?

Perhaps surprisingly, not really.

While the services that advertising companies like Google and Facebook provide us with feel, in the moment, like a fun escape, in the longer term, engaging with them becomes a Faustian bargain. Personalization algorithms lead us to become blissed out as we stimulate our mind, which further ensconces us in a dopamine-centered life over time.

This leads us to become even more anxious, as we experience fewer chemicals of calm and spend less time on activities that provide us with energy and satisfaction and are aligned to what we value.

## The Dopamine Bias

As I've mentioned previously, our brain craves novelty by default, and the more novel an experience is, the more dopamine our brain rewards us with.

To see just how novel the internet can be, as an experiment, try visiting your social network of choice and reflecting on how novel the posts you see are (how surprising and unexpected they are to you). If you've sworn off social media, try checking a news website instead. At the same time, do your best to not get sucked in to the app.

For example, visit Instagram, tap on your personalized Explore tab, and reflect on how novel the images you see are. If you're like me, it's going to be hard to not get sucked in and mindlessly scroll for a few minutes. If you visit Facebook or Twitter and catch a few news updates, hilarious memes, and articles that have let those in your social graph regain their "faith in humanity," reflect on how novel those updates are, too.

If you happen to get sucked in, consider how much control you really have over your attention when using personalized apps. On the internet, our intentions very quickly slip from our grasp.*

As you'll find, the most novel information on the internet appeals to our base fears, desires, and anxieties. And while this information stimulates us, it also drives us away from calm. Calm may bring us satisfaction, enjoyment, and relaxation. But in the moment, we rarely gravitate toward what provides it.

Instead, we gravitate toward dopamine, even when dopaminergic habits don't provide us with lasting meaning or genuine, deep enjoyment. It's hardly a choice when deciding between a stimulating scroll of Facebook and a quiet, contemplative cup of tea. We choose dopamine almost every time—a decision that's gratifying in the moment, but leads to a feeling of emptiness when we're finished.

I like to think of this as our brain's dopamine bias: we try to maximize dopamine in the moment, even if this makes us more anxious with time and works against our longer-term goals.

## The Three Dopamine Factors

The internet is chock-full of what scientists call superstimuli. In addition to the accomplishment mindset and the mindset of more, super-

---

* Social media also compromises human connection because it allows us to create a unique reality for ourselves by deciding whom we consume information from. Everyone's YouTube homepage is different—and uniquely novel to them. These "filter bubbles" of customized content can make it more difficult for us to relate to one another as we develop more polarized interests.

stimuli are a primary reason the modern world makes us feel so anxious.

I think of **superstimuli** as *highly processed, exaggerated versions of things we're naturally wired to enjoy*. They're artificial, more stimulating versions of the real thing—with the most desirable components cranked way up to produce more dopamine, which leads us to come back later for more. This is especially true when these stimuli are algorithmically tailored to be novel to *us*. Most superstimuli are found on the internet.

The modern world provides us with alternatives to activities that provide a more balanced release of neurological chemicals. A few examples:

- Checking social media is more stimulating than talking to a friend over breakfast.
- Pornography is more dopaminergic than sex.
- Ordering takeout from an app is more stimulating than cooking dinner with your spouse.
- Watching YouTube videos is more stimulating than reading an engaging book with a cup of tea.
- Lying on the couch reading the news online is more stimulating than exercising by going on a bike ride or walking around town.
- A Netflix marathon is more stimulating than playing board games with your spouse or making a living room fort with your kids.

Remember: when given a choice, we'll more often than not gravitate to what maximizes the release of dopamine. Superstimuli provide us with more dopamine than everything else we could be spending our time and attention on, even if that enjoyment is short-lived.

• • •

The more dopamine an activity releases in your brain, the more addictive the activity becomes with time. Research shows that three factors influence the size of the dopamine hit we get:

1. **Novelty.** How surprising and unexpected something is to us.
2. **Direct effect.** The extent to which a stimulus tangibly and directly influences our life, or how much it matters to us. This is also referred to as saliency.
3. **Genetics.** Some of us are simply predisposed to experience higher or lower dopamine levels in some regions of our brain.

Genetics is outside the scope of this book, but it's worth talking about briefly. This book covers a wide range of ideas and rituals for calm. It would be impossible to explore any one idea completely—the book would be twenty thousand pages long if we did, and nobody wants that. On top of this, when it comes to writing about the brain, usually some simplification is necessary. For example, while I'm focusing mainly on how dopamine overstimulates our mind, there's also a lighter side to dopamine: it helps us think, motivates us to make a difference, and lets us lead a more intentional life. On top of this, many habits that release calming neurochemicals also release some dopamine simultaneously. Dopamine is not all bad, especially when paired with chemicals of satisfaction. As with striving and savoring, it's all about balance.

Genetics can also illuminate a darker side of dopamine. There are numerous diseases and disorders associated with altered dopamine levels in the brain: Parkinson's disease, ADHD, and anorexia are all, at least in part, associated with lower levels. On the flip side, Tourette's syndrome, psychosis, and some addictions are associated with higher levels in some parts of the brain, or in the case of addiction, repeated dopamine surges. Schizophrenia and bipolar disorder are also often associated with dopamine imbalances.

While genetics plays a role, here's the thing to keep in mind: *your sources of dopamine matter enormously.* Calm habits release a balanced cocktail of chemicals, including dopamine. It's when habits release *primarily* dopamine that you risk getting into trouble.

This is especially the case with novel superstimuli.

I've already written about novelty, the first dopamine factor. We're presented today with more novel stimuli than we have ever seen in our human evolutionary history. Novel superstimuli numb us while simultaneously making us anxious. The more dopamine we get accustomed to living with, the more we desire maintaining that level of stimulation—and the less we'll feel calm in the here and now. It's the classic broadcast TV–to–YouTube flip: entertainment is no longer just novel in general, it's uniquely novel to *us.* This makes it more enticing— and harder to resist—than ever before.

Nowhere is this novelty more on display than on the most taboo of websites: internet pornography. Porn is an admittedly awkward, yet strangely fascinating, topic to write about. There are few internet services so prevalent in their usage, yet so forbidden as to even mention: 70 percent of men are regular users of porn, but few will talk about these websites.

In many ways, internet porn is the ultimate superstimulus. As Gary Wilson, the author of *Your Brain on Porn* has written, porn websites "build [the] pursuit of novelty into their layout, [because with] multiple tabs open and clicking for hours, you can 'experience' more novel sex partners every ten minutes than your hunter-gatherer ancestors experienced in a lifetime." Sexual arousal raises dopamine levels higher than almost anything else, so it's no wonder that internet porn—which is highly artificial but crucially more novel than actual sex—can be so addictive.

As with most superstimuli, porn is not without severe downsides. One study found that "after consumption of pornography, subjects reported less satisfaction with their intimate partners—specifically, with these partners' affection, physical appearance, sexual curiosity, and sexual performance." Rephrasing this study to sound less academic: porn can wreck the sexual intimacy in your life while making your partner less attractive to you. They're the same person—you just see them as less attractive. And this study was conducted in 1988, *before* the advent of pornography on the internet. Needless to say, these days the novelty factor is much, much higher. And so are the negative effects. Intimate time with your partner releases less dopamine than time spent on porn—and as a result, your primitive brain considers that time to be less valuable than it does some video on the internet. (The intimate time releases significantly more here-and-now chemicals.)

In many cases, porn usage can lead to anxiety and depression, perhaps because, as a superstimulus, it can make our mind more anxious and reliant upon dopamine. Much as social media simulates human connection yet leads us to less intimacy with our friends, porn mimics intimate connection, while making us less close with our partner or, if we're single, with potential romantic partners.

When we're not careful, even our deepest personal connections can become unfortunate casualties of our constant craving for novelty.

• • •

After novelty and genetics, the third dopamine factor is salience: the more of a direct difference a stimulus makes in your life, the more dopamine it will release. This factor is pretty straightforward. If you find a $20 bill on the ground and get a $5,000 per year pay raise in the same day, both events might actually be just as novel. But the pay raise will obviously make a far bigger difference in your life and lead to a more substantial release of dopamine as a result. Similarly, your partner saying yes to your marriage proposal will elicit a more significant dopamine spike than their agreeing to go on a fourth date with you.

The novelty factor comes into play here in a different way, too. It is sometimes said that a key to happiness is having low expectations. This is because of dopamine. If you expected a $5,000 pay raise and got it, you'd get a much smaller dopamine hit than if you didn't expect it.

Similarly, if you expected a $5,000 a year raise and received a one-time bonus of $1,000, you might feel disappointed—even though you're a thousand bucks richer.

This is because dopamine rises when something is better than expected and falls when our expectations aren't met. In our evolution, this function has served a purpose. As one study framed it, "situations in which rewards are unexpectedly obtained or withheld represent opportunities for new learning." When reality doesn't mesh with our expectations, we experience what neuroscientists call a "reward prediction error." This tells us that we're about to learn something valuable. By deconstructing what happened—and learning from the dopamine boost (or the lack thereof)—we can manage our expectations better the next time around. This helps us understand how the world works, heightening our chances of survival.

Unfortunately, superstimuli are built to exploit this learning loop.

## Taking Advantage

Personalization algorithms on the internet take advantage of both the novelty and direct-effect dopamine factors. As I've mentioned, the more information a data company collects about you, the more novel (to you) it can make your feed. On top of this, social networks are more addictive than other apps and websites because of how familiar they are to us: the content we see is about the people we know! It's hard to get more familiar than that.

Familiarity is, in large part, what makes internet superstimuli so addictive. When content is about a subject familiar to us, it becomes more attractive to us: it's friendlier, we feel less resistance to consuming it with repeated exposure, and we'll probably find it more enjoyable. In psychology, this is called the "mere exposure effect." When we're repeatedly exposed to any stimulus, we develop a preference for it simply *because* it's familiar to us. This is true regardless of whether a stimulus is positive, neutral, or negative. This could be why websites like YouTube funnel us into niches, topics that aren't just interesting but so personal that they become a part of who we are. By the sixty-seventh video about mechanical keyboards, the topic becomes a part of our identity and the stories we tell ourselves: we're no longer just loosely interested in keyboards, we're a mechanical keyboard *aficionado*. Subject familiarity is an accelerant for the consumption of novel information.

At the same time, digital dopamine drives us to maximize future resources through the mindset of more. Social networks provide us with metrics that our primitive brain deems more important than even money: metrics about how popular we are and how much we matter to the people we know. It is no wonder why so many of the apps operated by data companies have currencies associated with them: follower counts, Likes, and numbers of friends or connections are all examples of these kinds of currencies. Driven by dopamine, we feel the need to maximize most currencies that we come into contact with.

There is another, subtler way that data companies take advantage of our dopamine bias. When you open your impulsive app of choice, you may notice that you engage with content only around half of the time. Sometimes, the content is engaging enough to suck you in; the rest of the time, you bounce into and then right back out of the app. This may not be by chance: studies suggest that our brain releases about *twice* as much dopamine when there's a 50 percent probability of a reward, compared with when there's a 100 percent chance of one. It's no wonder we check email so often, and it's no wonder we keep coming back to social media apps.

As James Clear, the author of *Atomic Habits*, has written, "as a general rule, the more immediate pleasure you get from an action, the more strongly you should question whether it aligns with your long-term goals." We succumb to what Clear calls "exaggerated versions of reality" by falling victim to superstimuli "that are more attractive than the world our ancestors evolved in."

Our brain may desire calm, but it cannot resist dopamine.

Before continuing, it's worth reiterating the connection superstimuli have with calm. Much of our behavior online is driven by superstimuli, and the dopamine networks in our brain are anticorrelated with networks of calm. As a result, superstimuli drive us away from calm and toward anxiety. This makes the chemicals in our brain less balanced, by shifting activation in our brain away from networks that make us calm and present to networks that make us feel stimulated.

A key turning point in my own journey to find calm was when I realized that the apps on my phone were taking advantage of my brain's wiring. Like anyone, my mind loves (and craves) dopamine. I needed to tame this desire for dopamine, especially given my conflicting desires for focus, energy, and productivity.

Drugs are addictive because they lead to a dopamine spike in our brain. In this way, on a chemical level, Facebook, Twitter, and YouTube are identical to a lite version of an addictive substance. Only instead of causing a dopamine release in your brain through a pill, they release these same chemicals through audiovisual imagery that caters to our base emotions and impulses. This is not how we think of these services logically, but it's how our brain sees them primitively.

In the previous chapter, I briefly shared the story of getting my first iPhone, and how much of a wonder the thing was. As I spent more and more time on the device, it became more of a way to score hits of dopamine than a useful tool—it crossed the chasm of usefulness to become a negative presence in my day. Each year it was updated to provide an even more efficient hit: with bigger screens to deliver more information, faster processors to reduce how long I had to wait for dopaminergic apps, and better cameras to share a window into my life with the world to get more Likes.

It didn't help that I could use my phone to cater to whatever insecurities I had in each moment. If I wanted to feel a connection, I could check how many people liked a recent post on Twitter or Instagram. If I wanted some ego validation, I could check how many copies of my books sold that week through my publisher's author portal. If I wanted to feel accepted, I could text a few friends to see who messaged back first.

Of course, expectations skew reality: half of the time I was happy with the metrics, the other half of the time I felt let down. But I kept coming back. These metrics were an escape—even though, in practice, they were really just a hidden form of chronic stress.

## Stimulation Heights

Noticing how many superstimuli had crept into my life forced me to take a step back, to make a plan to eliminate the biggest distractions.

Deconstructing the reasons for my anxiety, I uncovered a bit of a messy picture. If you've made a list of your preventable sources of chronic stress, and have tried to tame the preventable ones, you may have found what I did. Despite my best efforts to tame sources of chronic stress, the superstimuli kept popping back up.

Of course, it takes time to rebalance our brain chemistry for calm. But superstimuli make this an uphill battle.

Looking back, as I had become more hooked on digital superstimuli, I had also grown to spend more time on analog superstimuli. Dopamine begets dopamine; the more dopamine we cause the release of, the more dopamine we crave, because we want to stay at that heightened level. The more I sought the chemical in the digital world, the more I desired it in my analog world. I drank more booze, ate more takeout, and did more shopping—online and off.

My days had started to orbit around the neurotransmitter without my realizing it. Sure, maybe I took a relaxing bath when I got to my hotel room—but only while listening to a podcast at the same time, after perhaps eating a delicious meal of butter chicken. And even if I disconnected when traveling, when the internet was an option on a flight, I'd often give in to the temptation of checking and connecting to get more hits.

Admittedly, I'm being a bit hard on myself in order to make a point. Unfortunately for me, while I performed well at work, setting aside the significant burnout episode, it was my personal life that was overrun with superstimuli, in the form of everything from apps I'd compulsively check to a good amount of processed takeout food every week.

This only served to drive me further away from calm.

Taking stock of our dopamine-driven habits is essential. Different activities have different "heights of stimulation" depending on how much dopamine is released when we tend to them. It's possible to visualize the activities we engage in, with the activities that release the least amount of dopamine at the bottom, and the actions that release the most at the top.

If you take stock of the activities you engage with throughout the day, and plot them in the illustration on the next page, you'll see that the most novel and personalized superstimuli live at the top, while your most boring activities live near the bottom. I've populated this chart with examples of stimuli I personally tended to throughout the week.

Of course, your illustration will look different—even if we both spend time on the exact same activities. We're all wired differently and find different levels of saliency and novelty in our daily tasks.

**The sum of dopamine released by your daily activities determines your overall stimulation height.** In this way, your level of mental stimulation is largely just a function of how much dopamine your mind is accustomed to living with.

If you spend most of your workday on email, social media, and the news, and come home to watch TV while drinking beer, you're going to live near the top of this chart—and feel pretty anxious as a result. You're also more likely to burn out if your distractions serve as sources of chronic stress.

Conversely, when you deliberately disengage from your most dopaminergic activities and find things to savor while noticing your engagement

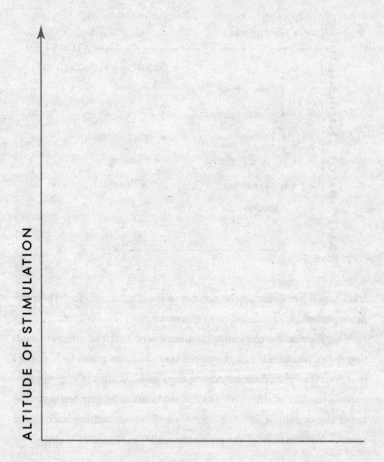

ALTITUDE OF STIMULATION

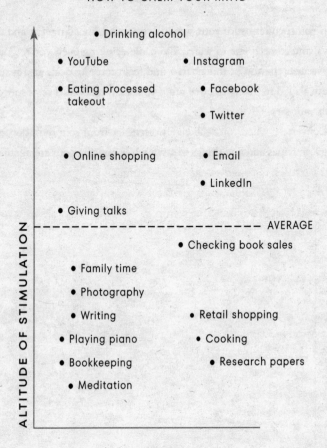

level, you'll live closer to the bottom of the illustration. You'll become more present, focused, and calm as a result.

This illustration obviously continues well past the arbitrary end-points I've identified. Past the upper bound of this graph lie activities that release an incredible amount of dopamine that few of us engage in, such as hard drug use. This fits the stimulation heights analogy: the larger the dopamine hit, the harder you'll come crashing back down after. Below the floor of the graph are activities that release almost no dopamine, which are hardly worth mentioning, like lying down awake with your eyes closed for several hours.

Between these endpoints are most of the activities you engage with daily.

I've found this chart to be a great way of visualizing my habits, tasks, and activities, to roughly observe how stimulated my mind is. I recommend charting your habits in this same way, with the most novel things you tend to at the top, and the least novel things you pay attention to at the bottom. You don't have to draw a fancy picture if you don't want to: just make a list of your daily activities and distractions, while minding how novel and salient each one is, to place it relative to the other ones on your list. I personally find the visualization helpful. Don't worry about getting your list perfect, just capture your activities and roughly how much dopamine each releases relative to the others, given how novel each item feels to you.

As a general rule, the more activities you engage with closer to the bottom of your chart, the calmer you will become.

Take stock of what superstimuli you fall victim to throughout the day—and notice your mind's impulse to stay at a high level throughout the day. For example, if you're working on a boring spreadsheet, do you keep your email client open in the background to continue flying at a high altitude? If you find yourself with a few spare minutes before a meeting, do you use that time to tap around on your phone? If you just landed after a disconnected plane ride, do you crave several hits of dopamine from your phone after going without them for several hours?

In sorting your daily activities by their height of dopamine release, and perhaps after a bit of experimentation, you may notice some of the same things that I did, including that:

- **Not all heights of stimulation are created equal.** The activities near the top of the graph are mostly a waste of time—these are the distractions and time wasters we often tend to out of the desire to stimulate our minds. These activities are often also a source of chronic stress. Beneath this band of activities are the tasks that allow us to fill our time with productivity and meaning and that provide a more balanced blend of neurochemicals. In this way, objects of attention lower down on this chart don't just lead to productivity and meaning—they help us feel happy and calm. They're also more active and less passive.

- **The higher you rise, the less you'll want to come down.** Dopamine is addictive—our mind has evolved to crave it and labels any behaviors that release the chemical as an activity that advances our goals. Our mind likes rising to a higher level of stimulation: we feel little resistance to paying attention to something more novel than what we're currently doing, like when we notice an email come in when we're working on a spreadsheet. It's much more difficult for us to move to a lower height. After all, doing so means giving up dopamine. In this way, there is a natural updraft in the illustration. This is a force that, in the modern world, we have to actively resist.

- **Your height of stimulation has probably risen over time.** Your average daily level of stimulation has probably increased with time, as the internet has burrowed its way into the gaps of your days.

- **The items on your chart are not static.** Some items on your illustration will rise with each passing year—generally speaking, the environments we find ourselves in are becoming more novel, not less. Certain things on your graph, like social media websites driven by personalization algorithms, may have risen substantially in recent years. As time marches on, the distance between digital superstimuli and analog stimuli increases.

- **Analog activities live near the bottom; digital activities live at the top.** This is not always the case: doing digital bookkeeping may live lower than attending a Broadway musical. Generally speaking, though, analog activities cluster at the bottom of the chart, while digital ones live closer to the top. While the analog activities we engage with usually lead to calm engagement, our digital lives are typically structured around maximizing the release of dopamine—which can bleed into our analog lives if we're not careful. This is a topic so important that I've devoted an entire later chapter to how we can better engage with the analog world (chapter 7).

- **What stimulates you does not necessarily make you happy.** In reflecting on the levels of your activities, you may find that those closer to the top and bottom of your graph engender very different feelings. If I had to describe the general tone I get from tasks near the top of my chart, I'd use words like "stressed out," "hollow," and "escape." I'd be inclined to use words like "enjoyment," "satisfaction," and "calm" with things near the bottom. This, again, is due to the neurochemicals that these different activities release.

Right now, I'm going to leave how to wean yourself off superstimuli as an "open loop" in your mind until you read the next chapter. As I found, it would take quite a bit of experimentation and research to tame the superstimuli that were growing like weeds through the cracks of my day.

For now, if you do decide to make your own Stimulation Height chart, please resist the urge to be hard on yourself. Keep in mind that craving dopaminergic activities is part of what makes you human. The awareness that this activity provides is the first step to changing your behavior for the better.

## The Key to Relaxation

Only staying active will make you want to live a hundred years.

JAPANESE PROVERB

I've devoted most of this chapter, not to mention this book, to discussing the forces that elevate us to new heights of stimulation and anxiety—including chronic stress, the accomplishment mindset, the mindset of more, and superstimuli. Through all of this, I hope you find that one neurological truth rings out louder than all of the others: that we've optimized our days around the wrong neurochemicals for being calm.

As the digital world has become more novel and salient, we've only spent more time in it, including when we are trying to relax. In this way, we don't spend our downtime nearly as fruitfully as we did in the past (assuming you didn't grow up with social media). Superstimuli lead us to become more anxious and less calm, more stressed and less present, and less mentally balanced as we seek out dopamine above all else. These same superstimuli also lead us to spend our downtime passively instead of actively.

We typically feel guilty when we relax, but this feeling of guilt is often just what we label the discomfort we experience when we adjust to a new, lower level of mental stimulation. We have different labels for the ways our mind squirms as we become mentally calm—boredom, restlessness, impatience, and guilt—depending on the nature of our thoughts.

It's all part of the process of finding calm.

Seeing the myriad ways that superstimuli made me anxious forced me to step back, take stock, and make a deliberate effort to use downtime to find a way to quiet my mind.

By using downtime to lower our height of stimulation, we reclaim calm. I would even go so far as to say that **lowering our average stimulation height is the *purpose* of downtime.** In this way, we're able to spend downtime in a way that genuinely calms our mind, instead of indulging in habits that are just hidden sources of anxiety. We can properly come down, and stay at a lower level, where calm lives. As with the canary in the coal mine, there's far more oxygen for us at these lower altitudes.

Look toward the bottom of your Stimulation Height chart. That's where you'll find satisfaction and calm.

What provides immediate gratification may release more dopamine. But when a stimulus is not immediate, it's more satisfying and releases a more balanced set of neurochemicals that allow us to ease more deeply into our life over time. While our mind gravitates to activities that have a high stimulation-to-effort ratio, this tendency usually leads to heightened anxiety. Resisting this impulse leads to greater levels of calm.

Calm lives where we become mesmerized by the fire while camping, or just notice the little things in our day; the changing colors of the trees we pass by on our morning commute, the sight of the sun as it peeks over the horizon line. The lower our stimulation height, the easier savoring everyday life becomes.

Spending more time at these lower heights will likely be the most challenging and rewarding thing you do on your journey to calm. Seeking an outlet for relaxation after a long day, we gravitate to super-stimuli to keep our mind at the same level: indulging in video games, social media, drinking, online shopping, and mindless internet surfing.

To truly unwind, we need to adjust downward.

Though it would require a substantial amount of effort in my own journey, I would eventually find ways to lower my stimulation height and find replacements for habits like these—ideas we'll cover in the next few chapters. This journey would also lead me to do what some call a dopamine fast—a story I'll cover now.

As gimmicky as the idea might sound, it works surprisingly well for finding calm.

## CHAPTER SIX

## Stimulation Fasting

Around a year into my journey to find calm, despite some lingering difficulties with letting go of superstimuli, my mission to find calm was progressing nicely. I had identified many of the problems underlying my anxiety: the accomplishment mindset, the mindset of more, and superstimuli had all led me to take on needless chronic stress as well as structure my days around the release of dopamine. Using many of the ideas I've shared so far, I was also making inroads into lowering my anxiety, taming burnout to become more engaged, and dealing with many of the sources of chronic stress left on my list.*

As I continued exploring the research related to finding calm, two additional lessons quickly became apparent.

The first is that while the practice of taming preventable sources of chronic stress lets us make significant headway toward finding calm, it's just as critical that we deal with *un*preventable sources of chronic stress. Our unpreventable sources of chronic stress are often just as numerous as those we can tame. Besides, our mind ultimately doesn't

---

* I say "many of the ideas" because I'm telling my story a bit out of order. I've structured this book around which tactics actually allowed me to make progress toward calm, instead of when I personally discovered them, to try to make the book more helpful.

know (or care) which sources of stress are preventable or unpreventable. Both boil over just the same.

It's important that we develop habits to become less fazed by unpreventable stress. Luckily, many forms of unpreventable chronic stress roll off our shoulders once we integrate proper stress-relief strategies into our life. The stress is still there—we simply have a renewed capacity to deal with it.

The second lesson, which is just as essential, is that we need to make a special effort to deal with our *stickiest* sources of stress—the superstimuli we find too alluring to resist. The worst superstimuli hook in to our mind to take advantage of the very ways in which our brain is wired. As with delicious cookies in the cupboard that you have to actively resist all day long, it can be challenging to resist superstimuli with pure willpower alone. Some structural change is needed.

In the next chapter, we'll target the stress we cannot prevent. In this one, let's zero in on the stress we *can* prevent, and tame those stubborn sources of superstimuli that keep popping back up, despite our best efforts to resist them.

## The Flow of Stress

The science behind stress suggests something curious: stress is something that can *build up inside of us* over time. When we don't relieve the pressure that this stress creates and relieve it frequently, it only builds further.

Visualize, for a second, a strong, pressurized steel drum, with a pipe entering into it. That pipe is designed to do one thing: feed scalding steam into the drum. The drum fills with steam when the spigot is flipped to the on position. As a result, it becomes more pressurized.

As you might have guessed, in this analogy, the strong container is your mind (and body), and the steam is stress.

This analogy works pretty well for visualizing the effects of stress—as well as the differences between chronic and acute stress. Acute stress is temporary but still feeds steam into the drum—we feel the additional pressure, even if only for a bit. In a life with *only* acute stress, we naturally and automatically engage in stress-relief strategies that let us, to use a fitting (and probably corny) analogy, let off some steam. As we go about our lives, we release stress by doing everyday stuff to unwind, like listening to podcasts, reading books, getting physical activity, and going on vacations.

In contrast, we never stop feeding chronic stress into the drum. The more chronic stressors we experience, the more steam we feed in, and the more pressure builds up. With an average amount of chronic stress—say, the pressure that comes from demands at work, running a household, or nagging financial concerns—we can manage just fine. We relieve enough pressure over time to feel stressed but remain present. This is especially the case when our stress originates from a pursuit of purpose in our life, when our efforts are connected with our values. It's when we add too many unnecessary sources of stress—like compulsive checks of online news, social media websites, and apps—that stress begins to accumulate at a greater pace than we release it. Over time, we edge closer to our personal burnout threshold.

If you've felt some of the negative effects of stress I've mentioned in the book, like burnout and anxiety, you've probably felt them because, like me, pressure has built up with nowhere to go.

Doing nothing, your pressurized drum starts to shake. *Anxiety.*

Doing nothing for a longer period of time, the pressure accumulates, until your drum comes apart at the seams. *Burnout.*

At this point, you may have no choice but to pick up the pieces and start over again.

Fortunately for us, there is a release valve on the drum: stress-relief strategies that serve to balance our minds. These tactics let off steam and reduce cortisol so stress can't accumulate to the point of adverse effect.

Here is another quick reflection question for you: Do you have more stress flowing into your life than out of it?

This is admittedly an impossible calculation to make, and you might not even know the answer. But if possible, get a rough handle on how well you're doing.

In this way, at the risk of my sounding like a dork,* managing our stress can be thought of as a "flow optimization equation." When we have too much stress flowing into our life, our drum starts to rattle, and then comes apart when enough unrelieved stress accumulates.

When the stress flowing into our life roughly equals that which flows out (the stress we relieve), we feel happy, energized, and engaged.

Not enough stress can also present a problem. Think back to the person at the unmotivated end of the productivity spectrum: when you have more stress flowing out than in, you may need to find sources of *worthwhile* stress, including new challenges to take on, lest you feel unmotivated just the same. Remember: good stress, often called *eu*stress (the opposite of *dis*tress), makes life surprisingly enjoyable and meaningful across the longer arc of time.

If you're anything like I was and have more stress flowing in than out, you must find ways of relieving the excess stress.

---

* Perhaps it's too late in the book for this.

To set up how we can do so, let me share a story of another experiment I embarked on, conducting what is often called a dopamine fast. If you have some dopaminergic sources of stress remaining—that you still can't resist for some reason—this tactic may help a surprising amount.

Along the way, we'll reconnect with a few exciting neurochemicals that will propel us closer to calm.

## Dopamine Fasting

Midway into my research for this project, despite all I had discovered about topics like calm, anxiety, and burnout, I was still a bit anxious and restless. Even though I had explored a good number of strategies for finding calm since the onstage anxiety attack, the reason for this lingering anxiety was apparent: I was having trouble taming my most superstimulating sources of chronic stress. Superstimuli like Twitter, Instagram, and news websites left me tired, cynical, and unproductive. In the moment, though, they were candy; sweet, but with a deeply bitter aftertaste.

Sure enough, as I've written in my previous books, if I didn't have a distraction-blocker app enabled while working, I fell victim to them. Off the clock, I didn't hold back either. Tough as this is to admit, I'd spend hours engaged with these sources of chronic stimulation some evenings.

Something had to give.

As I've mentioned, some simplification is often necessary when writing about our neurochemistry. This extends to the neurotransmitters in our brain, dopamine included.

While dopamine can addict us to superstimuli, the chemical isn't all bad. Dopamine can provide us with motivation, help us to think logically and long term, and even supports many of our body's routine operations, helping our blood vessels, kidneys, pancreas, digestive system, and immune system function. As anxious and unproductive as overindulging in dopamine can make us, we couldn't survive without it.

Because so many people find they're unable to release themselves from the chemical's grasp, many turn to the idea of conducting a dopamine fast (sometimes called a dopamine detox): abstaining from any behaviors driven by dopamine for a prespecified period in an effort to balance their mind. The name "dopamine fast" is a bit of a misnomer: we can't detox from dopamine any more than we can detox from carbohydrates.

But what we *can* step back from are the stimulating rituals that lead us to convenient and empty hits of dopamine—the ones for which a primary purpose of an activity is the dopamine spike itself. It is through this kind of detox—which I've come to think of as really more of a *stimulation* fast than a dopamine fast—that we may wean ourselves off impulsive behaviors motivated by the chemical while rooting out pathways in our brain that no longer serve us. (I'll refer to the experiment as a stimulation fast going forward.)

Some time into my journey to calm my mind, I decided to step back from as many artificial stimuli as possible for one month, to both try to settle my mind and limit how much chronic stress I was piping into my life. My aim was to decrease my stimulation height in a way that would last.

I began by making a list of the superstimuli that remained in my life, also thinking about the stubborn sources of chronic stress that I still engaged with, including when I did not want to. Then I made a plan to eliminate or reduce how often I tended to these distractions. Nearly all of the distractions I eliminated came from the busyness layer.

Some stimuli were related to work, others were personal. Some were digital, others were analog. It didn't matter: identifying as many dopaminergic, stimulating things as I could, I laid out the ground rules to follow, and did my best to anticipate obstacles ahead of time.

On the analog side, I cut out all alcohol (which provides a substantial dopamine rush), didn't order any takeout (a favorite highly processed escape of mine), and was mindful to not overeat, especially in response to stressful situations.

Most of the stimuli that I cut out, as you might guess, were digital. These felt oddly refreshing to tame. For starters, I eliminated all digital news for the month, including websites like *The New York Times*, CNN, *The Verge*, and *The Globe and Mail*. I used a distractions blocker called Freedom on my computer and phone, which prevented me from visiting these sites even if I wanted to, and deleted problem apps from my phone. While at it, I cut myself off from social media—Twitter, Instagram, YouTube, and Reddit included. I allowed myself one exception: watching yoga and workout videos on YouTube, as well as videos from my two favorite tech YouTubers, which I genuinely enjoyed and didn't watch impulsively.

I also tamed instant messages, limiting myself to just three checks of text and other instant messages per day. To help accomplish this, I made sure to disable visible notifications for messaging apps—except for a numbered badge on each app's icon, so I could see, at a glance, if I had new messages to deal with when it was time to check. (This also helped time when I did my three checks, after enough messages had built up.)

I also limited myself to three daily email checks. This was the most challenging part of the experiment to follow through with. To help, I enabled an autoresponder to let people know not to expect a response immediately. That, along with the distractions-blocker boundaries of the experiment, did the trick.

I also tamed digital stimuli that provided me with validation or an ego boost. For the month, I didn't tend to vanity metrics, including checking how many books I had sold every week, or how many people were visiting my website, downloading my podcast, or subscribing to my newsletter.

As the experiment went on, I also found it helpful to create a few other rules to live and work by:

- If I wanted to watch TV, a movie, or something on a streaming site, I had to decide twenty-four hours ahead of time that I'd do so, to not give in to impulse.
- If I wanted to send someone a message—whether over email or over text—I'd add the message to a text file on my computer, which was full of drafts of texts, emails, and instant messages to send off the next time I allowed myself to connect. This let me choose to engage with people—they couldn't interrupt me at random intervals throughout the day.
- If I bought something online, I had to know what I wanted before visiting the website, so I couldn't do any online "window-shopping."

At the same time that I shrank (or eliminated) these elements in my life, I began investing in activities to replace them that provided a more balanced release of chemicals. (If you're looking for calming activities that can replace your own sources of distraction, you're in luck: I've packed the next chapter full of them. These strategies also help you absorb stress.) This prevented a hole from existing in my schedule, where the old stress-inducing habits used to be.

## Chemicals of Now

Before getting to how the experiment went, it's time to say hello again to a few more characters that will accompany us on our journey to calm—the here-and-now chemicals: oxytocin, serotonin, and endorphins. As you read these words, each of these chemicals is coursing through your brain and body, helping you live your life and process what you're reading. As with the release of dopamine, how much of each chemical your brain and body release depends on genetics and what kind of activities you engage in throughout the day. In swapping out my dopaminergic habits, I wanted to make sure the activities I spent my time on led to a balanced release of these calm chemicals.

If you've read many popular psychology books, you've probably heard the names of these neurotransmitters before. For our purposes here, their names and the methods through which they function, while interesting, don't matter as much as how these chemicals make us feel. In short, they make us present, happy, and connected.

As a refresher, **serotonin** makes us feel important and happy (like when we hit a new goal weight or accomplish something we've been working toward); **endorphins** make us feel euphoric (like when we're in the zone during a workout); and **oxytocin** makes us feel connected with others (like when we get a massage or have intimate time with our partner). These chemicals, combined with others like dopamine and cortisol (our body's primary stress hormone), determine how we feel at any given moment.

Activities that aren't highly dopaminergic tend to stimulate the release of all of these chemicals in varying amounts.

For example, getting a massage is a way of stimulating the release of **oxytocin**. Any friendly activity that involves physical touch will also release the chemical. At the same time, other chemicals come along for the ride as a bonus: getting a massage has been shown to increase serotonin and dopamine levels while decreasing cortisol. In this way, you feel connected, happy, and less stressed. Similarly, volunteering is a way of boosting serotonin levels—while also releasing oxytocin, because of how it lets you connect with others. Of course, spending time with those we love is an excellent way of boosting oxytocin as well.

While oxytocin can be found in any activity that makes us feel physically and emotionally connected with others, **serotonin** is found in activities that make us proud. We also experience a serotonin hit when we feel superior to others. On the surface, this sounds like a bad thing—and it can be. A part of our mind constantly compares ourselves to others to see how we stack up—the same piece of us that wants to know what everyone does for a living. But setting status seeking aside, serotonin makes us feel happy and comfortable. We can stimulate its release by maintaining an accomplishments list, which I did throughout the fast, to remind myself what fruits my daily efforts led to. We also get a hit of this chemical whenever we feel like a "big fish in a small pond"—which reminds us of all we have to be proud of. For this reason, as I've mentioned, a surefire way to release serotonin is volunteering. We feel important because we witness ourselves making a difference. Serotonin also protects us from the damaging effects of cortisol. Curiously, while serotonin is often called the "feel-good" chemical, most of the serotonin in our body is found in our gut. (We'll explore food and calm in the next chapter.)

**Endorphins** are released whenever you experience physical pain, laugh, or cry. A good stretch also releases these. While I didn't make time to rewatch *The Notebook* or reread *The Time Traveler's Wife* during the fast, I did make sure to carve out plenty of time for exercise and spent more time with friends I could laugh with. If you do a stimulation fast, be sure to get plenty of exercise: not only does it release endorphins, it leads to the release of dopamine. This can help your mood if your dopamine dips at the beginning of a stimulation fast. Exercise can also lead to the release of endocannabinoids, making us feel calm and at ease—such as when we achieve a runner's high. Another way of getting a dose of every here-and-now chemical is making love. According to research, almost nothing makes us more present than intimate time with a romantic partner.

Dopamine is also worth focusing on as it relates to calm. Again, the sources from which we derive dopamine deeply matter. A life propelled primarily by dopamine feels less meaningful. During the experiment, I still found myself engaging in dopamine-releasing behaviors, but I made sure to obtain my dopamine from cleaner-burning sources. I spent a fair amount of time planning and doing creative work, both of which are supported by the brain's dopamine system. Any activity that's difficult and requires effort to do releases dopamine (just less than more convenient sources). Most of us have enough of these activities in our life that we don't need to go out of our way to find them. Disengaging from the dopamine that comes from stimulation and replacing that with dopamine sourced from engagement is one of the best trades you can make for your mental health.

Here's the thing to keep in mind: **any activity that leads you to**

**enjoy the present moment will lead you to experience greater calm.** This, as a result, will make you more engaged, productive, and satisfied.

> If you find that something still feels off after carving out time for activities like these, you may need pharmacological assistance in order to find calm. That's okay. While medical advice is beyond the scope of this book, be sure to talk to a psychiatrist if you still need a hand after trying out these ideas. Be sure to also get medical guidance before conducting a dopamine fast if you experience severe withdrawal symptoms when abstaining from more extreme dopaminergic habits (like drug use).

## A Bunch of Curious Lessons

In short, a stimulation fast can be considered a shortcut to balancing or even rebooting your mind.

One of the first discoveries I made after I kicked off the experiment was just how much time I spent in the busyness layer; on compulsive checks, mindless scrolls, and mind-numbing taps. Cutting out these checks, I immediately found myself with more time to spend on activities that helped me find more balance. I invested in the tactics in the next chapter, spending more time in nature, exercising more often, and cooking fun and elaborate meals (including a killer angel food cake my wife still talks about). I also meditated more—one of the best ways of activating the here-and-now network, according to Daniel Lieberman, the coauthor of *The Molecule of More*, whom we met a couple of chapters ago. I invested in my learning, read more books, and, in the digital world, listened to audiobooks and podcasts and took a couple of online classes. To connect with others, I spent more time volunteering, hanging out with friends, and, of course, annoying my wife. I made room for creativity, too: taking an improv class, painting, and learning how to play the piano. At work, I had more time to write, explore research, and interview people to discover more about calm. I paid less mind to what was instant and stimulating, and more mind to what was productive and important.

Even as someone who studies time management for a living, I was surprised by how much more free time I had. We tell ourselves that we have very little free time—but we have far more of it than we think. Our distraction time is sprinkled throughout our day *between* our more meaningful experiences, but all that time really does add up.

We have the time for activities that make us calm. The reality is that we don't have the *patience* to adjust to a lower stimulation height.

The stimulation fast is really a way of forcing yourself to be patient, to fly at a lower altitude. I found the results of this experiment can materialize surprisingly quickly—within a matter of days. And contrary to what you might expect, the experiment can even be fun, especially when you decide, ahead of time, which activities to sub in for your most stimulating habits. The experiment will prove a challenge. But, engaged with activities that induce a meaningful calm, you won't notice it nearly as much as your mind settles down. (I personally find that one month is a reasonable length of time over which to conduct this kind of fast. That might feel long, but the idea is to make lasting changes, and for this, a longer time period can help. Adjust this duration for what works for you: if less of your day revolves around dopamine, you may need a shorter duration of time for the reset.)

On top of the extra free time, I found that I focused on more fruitful things—my work time became more productive, and my personal time became more meaningful, almost immediately. Finding myself on a work break on the first day of the fast, instead of refreshing the news, I organized the receipts on my desk, which had been piling up for a while. After work, because scrolling through news updates on my iPad wasn't an option, I had to look for better alternatives if I wanted to occupy my mind, like calling up a friend or doing something on my savor list. The part of my mind that continually considered the opportunity cost of my time had fewer options—but the options it did have were productive and meaningful. Another quick win.

Within a couple of days, my energy also rose. This happened, I believe, for two reasons. First, I invested in habits that led to a more balanced mind. I was happier and more engaged, and had more energy at my disposal to tackle each day. Second, I was no longer feeding my mind chronic stress by repeatedly checking the same set of websites. The effect of this, as well, was near instant: on the second day, instead of mindlessly reading email on my phone after waking up, finding myself with a few minutes, I picked a book up off my nightstand and read it for ten or fifteen minutes. When it came time to respond to the messages that had come in, I didn't reread the same ones several times before responding: I was only allowed three checks and just calmly answered what had come in.

A week into the experiment, I decided to add back one weekly check of how my business was performing, checking metrics like book sales and speaking requests. I figured this could let me stay true to the spirit of the experiment of lowering my stimulation level, without burying my head in the sand and ignoring valuable information. Sure enough, it worked, in an unexpected way: I could zoom out from the random daily blips in statistics to see broader, overall trends in my business.

This is the case for any metric you have in your life: the less often you check your own numbers, the more you can zoom out to obtain a broader perspective. By stepping back from our habits, we gain perspective on them. For example, by checking your investment account balances every month instead of every hour, you're able to see the wider trend lines of how your accounts are performing, instead of overreacting to every daily fluctuation that will be smoothed out by time. If you lead a sales team, receiving a weekly sales update instead of compulsively refreshing your team's sales portal will let you differentiate between short-term fluctuations and longer-term trends. If you run your company's social media accounts, instead of learning about every new follower that comes in, you can zoom out to find trends just the same—maybe you're even *losing* followers as time goes on!

The more you zoom out, the more perspective you get about what actually matters.

Curiously, another way that I was able to gain perspective related to the information I consumed online. The internet is a polarizing place because, much like with the most niche videos on YouTube, strong opinions are algorithmically rewarded on social media. After all, they're the most novel voices, which lead to the most engagement and time spent in our social media apps of choice. Checking the news and social media less often, I found that I experienced less chronic stress because I was exposed to less threatening information on a regular basis. Another reason our digital world provides us with chronic stress is that it broadens what I think of as our *surface area of concern*, which is the scope of events we pay attention to regularly.

Before radio, TV, and the internet came along, we had to subscribe to a newspaper to know what was happening outside the boundaries of our life (as well as the lives of those we care about). We experienced far less chronic stress from events that did not directly affect us. This is not to say that we had *no* stress, but we did have less to worry about that was outside our control.

An expanded surface area of concern is not inherently a bad thing. Knowing about adverse events leads us to mobilize to make things better. Plus, our ability to empathize with others is one beautiful part of what makes us human. But all of this is worrisome as it relates to anxiety, especially as far as our news consumption is concerned. The news is overwhelmingly negative, simply because we pay more attention to negative stories. One study found that negative news stories lead us to become more emotionally aroused, attentive, and reactive even on a *physiological* level. (In this same study, positive news had no observable effect.) When we're shown negative stories, we become more likely to click, tune in, and subscribe. Another study that analyzed weekly newsstand sales of the Canadian magazine *Maclean's* found that negative covers sold around *25 percent more copies* than more upbeat covers. In other words, buyers *chose* negative news over positive news. Our negativity bias takes over when we consume information, and we experience more chronic stress as a result. We get hooked on content that makes us feel *worse*. This tendency is worth being mindful of, especially during a stressful time, when a more significant proportion of the population is likely to be burnt out. Given cynicism is a core attribute of burnout, consuming information while in this state can skew our perspective of world events further. Remember your mind's negativity bias, and the fact that you experience around three positive events for each negative one.

Events that don't touch your life or affect those you care about or the communities you serve—particularly events that are outside of your control—are generally not worth tending to. Deliberately consuming less digital information helps you shrink your surface area of concern, which leads you to be exposed to less chronic stress. In all of these ways, stepping back will help you settle your mind while letting you connect with issues that affect your life.

Another benefit I discovered was how *quickly* I was able to lower my height of stimulation—and how my mind didn't put up as much of a fight with this as I thought it would have. Going into the experiment with alternative activities in mind, I reset my palate for mental stimulation. Research suggests that superstimuli become less novel to us with repeated exposure—and that, as we get desensitized, we engage with sources of stimulation more often, and seek out increasingly novel stimuli. Thankfully, going without your most stimulating distractions for a while makes even smaller amounts of pleasure satisfying.

When you cut out sugar, while you may struggle at first, within a couple of weeks your taste buds reset, and a ripe peach can taste just as delicious as a bowlful of Skittles. Stimulation is the same. If you're finding it challenging to savor the little things, you probably need to cut back.

A primary reason that superstimuli lead us to feel numb is that the reward pathways in our brain are designed for a world of scarcity, not abundance. During our evolutionary history, we obviously did not have access to an endless supply of dopamine as we do today. This abundance is not a bad thing in and of itself—but our brain *responds* to all this novel stimuli in a negative way. The more dopaminergic habits we repeatedly engage in over time, the less dopamine our brain produces as a response. In this way, stimuli that are fun at first eventually numb us. Just as someone who's addicted to pornography has to consume increasingly novel content to experience the same rush, so do consumers of social media, the news, and even highly processed junk food.

When something is scarce, our brain perceives it as valuable. When it's abundant, our brain expects it and calibrates back to our previous baseline level of happiness, a phenomenon called *hedonic adaptation*.

This same idea applies to savoring. Having less of something leads us to savor it *more*. Scarcity makes our experiences more valuable. Think of when you're eating a delicious cinnamon bun: your enjoyment per bite will not be consistent. It's likely pretty high for the first bite when the taste is most novel, then dips for the middle bites, then spikes again as you near the *final* bite—you'll be done eating it soon, so your brain figures you might as well enjoy the thing. This idea has been replicated in research. In one study, participants who received fewer pieces of chocolate than they expected to "ate more slowly, paid more attention to the experience, and showed increased levels of satiation, relative to [a control group who was told] they would receive a larger quantity but actually received the same number of chocolates" as the first group. In another study, participants who abstained from chocolate for a week savored an additional new piece even more. This is the scarcity effect in action. This could be why the wise, legendary investor Warren Buffett, who is worth more than $100 billion at the time of writing, clips coupons and lives in a house that he bought for $31,500 in 1958, about $250,000 in today's dollars. He's likely figured all this out. As he has put it, "I'd move if I thought I'd be happier someplace else."

We get used to what we enjoy, and abundance does not guarantee enjoyment. This is especially the case as far as dopaminergic superstimuli are concerned.

Shortly into the experiment, I became oddly excited about reading the paper every morning—my only source of news. Occasionally, when I heard those in my life talking about a news story the day before, I'd spring out of bed the following morning to walk to the doorstep to fetch the paper and get up-to-date. Just as a good way to lose weight is to feel a bit hungry before each meal, a path to savoring is to feel a sense of anticipation before enjoying something. While the front-porch news was a few hours old, each morning I found that this temporal space made me less reactive and gave me perspective on issues that mattered.

As the month progressed, with little time to spend on immediately rewarding stimuli, the experiment became one about depth, as much as one about dopamine. With some time to spare in the digital world, I revisited old webcomics that I hadn't read in years, laughing at them just the same. Later on, halfway into the experiment, my wife was out with a couple of friends, and I found myself lying on the couch, bored— a feeling I hadn't felt in a long time. It was then that I opened up the Photos app on my iPad and started to look through memories from years ago, when I had first moved away from home and was figuring out living life on my own. My now wife hadn't yet entered into the picture, and I was living in a small, sparsely decorated apartment in the city's Italian district. Seeing these photos made me feel nostalgic, reminiscent as I savored the past, in a way I had never felt. This also gave me some space to reflect on how lost I felt, and how I looked to the world with longing and reflection back then. Seeing our life from the rear-view mirror, we see things as more straightforward than they were, holding the knowledge of how our life's narrative will unfold.

That's when a simple idea hit me: longing for the past in this episode of nostalgia, I realized I wasn't longing for the life I had. I was longing to *relate* to my life in the same way as before. I didn't want to live in a sparsely decorated bachelor-sized apartment: I wanted the calm, to see my life as less complicated than it felt on the anxious end of the calm spectrum. Poking through old photos, I reached out to a few friends in them, and in every case, they were delighted to hear from me. It felt great to engage with them over the phone, instead of through some app that tricked us into trading dopamine hits with one another. I also gave my wife a gigantic hug when she got home, grateful to have her in my life (while also thankful she knows how to decorate the walls).

There seems to always be a part of us that longs for the past and sees the present as more complicated than it is, simply because we don't yet have a proper perspective. This makes sense: it's most difficult to zoom out from the present. This nostalgia feeling is a good one—and it was a gift to be able to connect with it during the experiment.

I would never have reconnected with these memories, experienced these serendipitous moments, or reflected on my past in this way if I had fired up Twitter instead. This is not to even mention the savoring I did for the future. With more time and attention between meaningful moments, my mind wandered more often to exciting upcoming events I eagerly anticipated. I savored them more as a result, too.

If I'm honest, I was surprised by how well the experiment worked. The idea of a so-called stimulation fast sounds gimmicky—but the technique can produce profound results. As the month went on, the busyness layer of my life continued to wither. I began to appreciate how the fast led me to have more of the ingredients I've mentioned: time, patience, productivity, meaning, perspective, calm, and depth. I also had more memories available to me, because of how I could process what happened in front of me in each moment.

But it wasn't just that I could process what was happening in my life. In settling my mind and connecting with calm, I found the patience for what unfolded in front of me.

Oh man, what a gift that was.

The experiment wasn't all sunshine and rainbows, mind you: during the first two weeks, old compulsions took time to fade away, as they will for you, if you decide to do a similar experiment (and you should). At the start, you may find that your mind is restless and craves distraction. You may also notice all of the various cues that lead you to pick up your phone: stressful situations, awkward moments, or feeling a bit bored. Notice all that you can, and remember that this restlessness is part of the process. What feels like restlessness is really just your mind calming down.

You may hit the odd snag along the way, and that's to be expected—just adjust as you go. After noticing that I habitually started looking at new message notifications each time I unlocked my phone, I started leaving the device in another room. My wife and I also bought a house toward the end of my very first stimulation fast—and there was a crazy amount of traffic cop–type work to do, coordinating between inspectors, brokers, and lawyers ahead of our closing date. (Purposefully and deliberately setting a timer to enter what I called "comms mode" helped me to compartmentalize this communication so I could disconnect and focus the rest of the time, outside of these sprints.) Then there were the urges—to order takeout, check metrics, or join my wife in a drink after an exceptionally long day. These proved nothing more than surmountable annoyances. Having alternatives to focus on helped immensely. I'm happy to report that I succumbed to temptation just once in the month, checking how well a book was selling when a couple of interviews came out about it.

Given how fruitful the experiment was, it was easy to call it a win.

## Conducting a Stimulation Fast

As you have probably gleaned, the steps to structuring a stimulation fast are straightforward; the more challenging part is in the follow-through. After my initial fast, I'd conduct a few more, each time in response to superstimuli creeping back into my life. This may be your rhythm, too. Because problem distractions take advantage of our neurological wiring, we need to tend to distractions that grow back. The key, as always, is awareness: check up often on whether stimulating distractions find their way back into your life, and when they do, set aside a month, or a few weeks if that's what you can spare, to step away from them once again.

Here are the steps I'd recommend to conduct a stimulation fast of your own.

- **Identify dopaminergic activities and distractions to weed out.** Look through both your analog and digital lives to get a feeling of what your most significant time and attention sinks are, which sources of distraction drain you the most. Make a list of all of the ones you want to cut out or reduce, while dealing with the dopaminergic habits on your stress inventory. Be sure to calibrate the experiment to your own life, and be realistic about which distractions you'll be able to prevent from arising. If you find it difficult to resist the allure of dopaminergic distraction throughout the day, define concrete boundaries around your fast. You can do so by downloading a distractions blocker on your computer; deleting problem apps from your phone (or changing your passwords to something so long and forgettable that you'll need to reset them to log in); or asking your spouse to become an accountability partner for the duration of the experiment (or better yet, to do one with you).
- **Identify and adopt more well-rounded activities.** This step is key and lets you replace your largest sources of chronic stress with shorter-lived sources of acute stress. To connect with chemicals of calm, identify some activities that promote presence through connection, accomplishment, and challenge. These

activities are usually found in the analog world, as I'll cover in the next chapter. Write down fun activities that make you present, including ones you haven't engaged with in a while because of a "lack of time." Reading and exercise are on many people's lists, and yours might also include calling old friends, playing a sport, painting, picking up a long-forgotten instrument, or gardening. Turn to this list whenever you're looking for something to do. The more substitute activities you identify, the easier this experiment becomes.

- **Choose a duration, conduct the experiment, and notice what changes.** The most helpful wellness strategies are self-reinforcing: you see they are working and thus become more likely to stick with them. This experiment is no different. After choosing a time period to do it for—I'd recommend at least two weeks, as it takes our mind around eight days to begin to settle into a new, lower level of stimulation—notice what changes. Do you feel calmer? Are you able to focus more deeply, and accomplish more at work? Do you become more present and invested in your personal life? Are you starting to feel less burnt out, stressed, and anxious? Make time to reflect on what changes occur and the differences the experiment makes.

## Reconnecting

My first dopamine fast occurred later on in my journey to calm, and as chance would have it, the fast ended mid-March of 2020—the start of the historic COVID-19 pandemic. This obviously made reconnecting to my sources of distraction after the experiment all the more distracting and anxiety inducing. While I kept on top of what was happening through the daily newspaper, reading updates online felt . . . different. It was the same news, only presented in a more extreme and concerning way. With a daily newspaper, I was able to find perspective. Online, I found only panic.

The loudest voices broke through to the top of my feeds, and I almost instantly felt like I had more to worry about—often while nothing materially changed in my life or in the lives of my loved ones following our first lockdown. The worries and concerns of everyone I encountered online became my own worries and concerns. Instead of only reading news updates from the calm, analytical perspective of a daily newspaper once a day, I read about the virus, stock market shocks, and political unrest from websites and feeds that refreshed every few *minutes*. I got caught up in the cyclone, the fray of worry, anxiety, and distraction that characterizes online social news activity.

At this point, I had an impulse that I had never had before: to step back. To disconnect. To no longer put my mind and heart in the hands of social networks to manipulate, distract, and take advantage of me for monetization purposes. Reflexively, on this particular day, I wrote a few fragmented words in the notepad on my desk that I use throughout the day:

> Twitter empties my soul
> The news empties my heart
> Both produce a threat response
> Cause burnout
> I need to avoid at all costs.
> They're minefields for me.

After my first stimulation fast, the stress that I had once found addictive had become empty and kind of pointless. At the time, I had enough stress just thinking about the health of my family, my business, and my city. There was no need to pile on the concerns of an overanxious world, and I was privileged in my ability to disconnect. This is not to discount the genuine pain others felt during the pandemic—we all have our own pandemic story, and some are far harder than others. But the takeaway here is simple: it's worth becoming mindful of our information diet during times that are particularly anxious and stressful. By doing so, we can stay calm, protect our mind, and hang on to the critical mental resources we need to actually engage with events as they unfold around us.

Often the lessons we most need to take to heart are the ones we, for whatever reason, have to learn a few times before they stick. In introducing and removing distraction from my days, I came to relearn one of those lessons: distraction begets distraction. This is because dopamine begets dopamine—the more stimulated we make our mind, the more stimulation we crave, all so we can continue flying at that height. For this reason, if we start the morning on a note of calm—with a book, a quiet cup of coffee, or waking up with our family—we're far more likely to find calm throughout the day.

There is no need to fly at such a high stimulation level. And there is definitely no need to let the news empty your heart.

## Fish Out of Water

If you were to cut down a tree and take a look at the trunk, you'd discover a series of concentric layers of rings inside, each a result of one growing season. These rings will tell you a story: of how old the tree is (count the rings to find the age), how much it grew each year (wider rings indicate more productive growing seasons), and even how crowded the tree was in its life (thinner rings on one side indicate the years it was cramped).

Our mind is similar: by looking at how our brain is structured, we can learn where we came from and understand more about our evolutionary history. We can learn, for example, that we are rewarded for being social—a good amount of our brain's structure is devoted to connecting with others. We can observe that the outer layers of our brain—such as the neocortex, which is responsible for logical reasoning, spatial reasoning, and language—evolved after the older, more instinctual parts of our brain that reside at the core of our mind, like the impulsive limbic system. This part often wins out when these systems have competing goals—like losing weight and eating a delicious pastry.

Despite the sophistication of our brain's outer layers, it's still very primitive at its core. The best evidence suggests that it reached its current state around two hundred thousand years ago. This might sound like a long time—and relative to the development of our modern world, it is. Relative to the time span of our brain's evolution, however, it's a mere blip.

Our brain evolved to its current state well before the modern world came into existence. In a way, it's a relic—while the speed of computers roughly doubles every two years, our brain has remained the same since we began hunting, gathering, and making tools with our hands. We hunted insects, reptiles, and birds while gathering berries, nuts, and vegetables. We turned rocks into knives, lit fires with flint, and stuck tree branches together to create shelter from the elements.

Today, we're forced to use this same primitive brain to live in a world that is unrecognizable to it. We're akin to a fish out of water, doing our best to get by. I'm not going to dig too deep into how our primitive brains aren't wired to thrive in the modern world—enough books do that, including one or two of my own. But it is worth reflecting on the fact that the brain you're using to read these very words formed during periods when nearly all of the stress we experienced was physical. We were hunted down by prey, ran from enemies, and were far more afraid of saber-toothed tigers than make-believe "electronic mail" arriving on the shiny, rectangular screen in our pocket.

Our primitive brains have two primary challenges in navigating the modern world. They face more stress than ever before, and have few outlets to shed that stress.

Today, most of our stress is mental—it doesn't exist in our physical world. And we let it build up inside of us, because we don't give it a place to go. Exercise used to be an outlet for stress—we walked an average of thirteen kilometers a day. Social connection used to be another outlet—we spent nearly all of our time surrounded by other people. We also used to put good, real food into our bodies—the stuff that grows in the ground and on trees and in bushes. Today, we move a fraction of what our bodies are wired for, and get less social interaction and eat less healthfully than ever before.

In a way, this can be okay—we can still live long lives thanks to trappings of the modern world, including healthcare, fast modes of transportation, and websites that simulate social interaction. But unfortunately, as you have probably found, the streams of stress flowing into our life far outnumber those flowing out. We have more email and less play; more social media and fewer hobbies; more "friends" and fewer deep connections. We spend more time watching the news than we do moving through nature; more time sitting and less time seeing into the eyes of our friends, family, and acquaintances.

More stress streams in, while less streams out.

Luckily for us, we can connect with how our brain and body are wired, while at the same time relieving stress and finding calm. A few of the primary ways we can do so are through people, movement, meditation, and good nutrition. These areas of our life all balance our mind, leading us to calm.

Curiously, these aren't just enjoyable activities to sub in for your dopamine habits. They also all exist in the same place: the analog world.

## CHAPTER SEVEN

*Choosing Analog*

Each day, we divide our time and attention across two worlds: the analog and the digital.

It's worth making a distinction between these two environments because they influence our lives in vastly different ways. Finding calm in the physical, analog world is far easier. Because the digital world is simulated and highly dopaminergic, it can upheave the balance of the neurotransmitters in our brain. Activities in the analog world, on the other hand, lead to the release of a more balanced mix of neurochemicals; they actively engage us with the present moment while leading us to greater calm. The analog world is also the environment that our ancient, two-hundred-thousand-year-old brain is designed for—the more time we spend in it, the better we feel. There are exceptions to this, of course: for this reason, we need to take the parts of both worlds that lead us to calm, meaning, and productivity, and leave much of the rest behind.

Many of us now spend far more time in the digital world than the analog one. In late 2019, the average American spent over ten hours per day tending to their digital lives. This measurement was taken pre-pandemic, before lockdowns, quarantines, and stay-at-home orders would intensify our relationship with the digital world. More recent data from the pandemic shows that our screen time has spiked to around *thirteen hours a day*—though it's tough to tell whether this rise is temporary or an early sign of an increasingly digital future. Note that these figures account only for the time we spend *looking* at screens; they don't include the time we are otherwise connected to the digital world, like when we're listening to a podcast or an audiobook.

These statistics should give you pause as someone whose brain is not built to thrive in the digital world. Actually, more than this, these numbers should frustrate you. The analog world is where we have historically lived; where we socialize with others, create things with our hands, enjoy the wonders of nature, and otherwise settle down and recharge. Calm lives in the analog world. But in the moment the digital world is so appealing, attractive, and molded to what we instinctually love, that we choose it instead.

When in doubt, we gravitate to what's stimulating.

Both worlds have their surprising benefits and drawbacks. While it's increasingly apparent that the digital world is not all it's cracked up to be, the truth is more nuanced: the analog world isn't all that it's cracked up to be either.

Let's dig in to both worlds to look at the ways they can add value to our lives in our journey to calm.

## Digital Wonders

I've been pretty hard on the digital world so far, and for good reason. Not only do most superstimuli reside in the digital world, but the digital world can also lead us to construct our days around the pursuit of more: giving us more to do, more to keep up with, more to worry about, and more "currencies" to accumulate. It can even fuel our accomplishment mindset, because we spend so much of our digital time keeping up with inboxes of all shapes and sizes, continually stressing about emptying them all to get to a state of *done*.

But it would also be ridiculous to dismiss the utility of the digital world. It gives us unprecedented opportunities for connecting to others. An increasing number of us work solely in the digital world, doing digital labor. If you do knowledge work, the proportion of your daily tasks that you do digitally has probably gone up with time—you make and deliver your contributions through the digital world. Outside of work, we remain connected to this world, too. The digital world is awesome, in the truest sense of the term. Just yesterday afternoon, I tapped on a glass screen a few times, and twenty minutes later, a piping-hot burrito showed up at my doorstep. Explain *that* to your two-hundred-thousand-year-old ancestor.

Just as an entire book can be written about how technology exploits our psychology, a book could be written about the wonders of the digital world. It can provide us with the motivation to become fitter—the same psychology that makes social media addictive can make a fitness subscription service feel like a fun game. The internet—which is inseparable from our digital lives—connects us with loved ones around the world: we even see their faces, live, a technology that would have been considered an unfathomable reality not too long ago. And our digital devices give us access to countless entertaining things: memes, kitten pictures, recipes, maps, and the ability to download any book, audiobook, TV show, or movie in a fraction of a second. And as long as there's a smart speaker somewhere nearby within listening distance, we get answers to random questions we ask out loud. Computing has become ambient; we no longer need to remember that there are 2.2 pounds in a kilogram. There are also a lot of pictures of turtles eating strawberries on the internet, which you will not regret searching for.

Despite all the needless stimulation this world can provide, it is truly a wonder.

This dichotomy of usefulness does lead to a question, though: if some elements of the digital world make us anxious, and others help us, how can we identify the parts of our digital world worth keeping, while cutting back on the rest?

Here's a simple rule to keep in mind: **the digital world is valuable only so far as it supports us in what we intend to accomplish.** Remember: at its best, productivity is about intention. That thirteen hours of screen time is not all bad; it's just unhelpful if it leads us to lose grip of our intentions.

Because the internet is so dopaminergic, our intentions quickly slip away from our grasp. We open a social media application to post something, but quickly switch to mental autopilot mode as we surf through other updates, sorted by most to least novel. The news is similar. Poking around on our news websites of choice, we get drawn to trending stories that are even more novel and stimulating than what we truly want to read. Visiting YouTube to search for a tutorial on how to replace the living room thermostat, we get sucked in to another novel video on our personalized homepage. Half an hour later, we forget why we visited YouTube in the first place until we set down our phone and notice the wires hanging out of the wall.

This doesn't always happen. But it happens enough to make us feel guilty about how we spend our time online after we notice ourselves falling in to these time traps.

The most supportive digital services do the opposite of hijacking our intentions: they support what we want to accomplish. When we tap on the Uber icon to summon a car, there are few distractions in-app to draw us away from that purpose (at least at the time of this writing). The same is true for countless others: apps we use to do guided meditations, meet up with other people, or follow along to guided workouts. Typically these services are less dopaminergic.

The best parts of the digital world serve as value adds to our analog environment. This is especially true when a digital service:

- **saves us time** (e.g., booking travel, getting directions, or messaging someone we're about to meet up with);
- **adds *features* to our analog lives** (e.g., calling an Uber or minding our activity with a fitness tracker so we can compete with friends); or
- **connects us with others** (e.g., dating apps and meetup websites).

These attributes of this world make our lives more streamlined and efficient, which lets us carve out more space for calm. They also lead us to spend our time more intentionally.

## Dividing Your Digital and Analog Lives

It is possible for us to further divide the activities we do into a Venn diagram of sorts, splitting our daily activities into three groups:

- **Digital-only activities.** We can only do these activities in the digital world, like refreshing our social media accounts, playing video games, and checking for new email.
- **Analog-only activities.** Activities we can only do the analog way, like taking a shower, sleeping, and drinking coffee.
- **Activities we can do in both worlds.** Examples of these activities abound, and include reading, managing money, playing games, practicing calligraphy, fetching our boarding pass,

coloring, navigating a map, journaling, using a stopwatch, and talking to friends.

Here's the trick to this advice: **when we want to do an activity efficiently, we should do it digitally, and when we want our actions to be meaningful, we should do things the analog way.** This way, we can use the internet for what it's good at—saving us time, adding features to our lives, and connecting us with others—while avoiding pesky digital rabbit holes.

If you've followed the activities in the book so far, you've probably already found a better balance to how you do your tasks. By taming the problem superstimuli in your life—cutting out sources of chronic stress and stepping away from the rest—digital activities that remain are more likely to support your intentions. You've likely also reconnected with a few analog activities, if you've enjoyed some items on your savor list, or subbed some analog activities into your life during the stimulation fast. With a calmer mind, you likely also don't crave internet superstimuli nearly as much.

But we can take this advice even further, deliberately doing tasks the analog way—especially ones that straddle the digital-analog divide.

## Analog Substitutes

Your fondest memories are likely analog: family road trips, deep conversations, and vacations to far-flung places. The digital moments—the ones you remember, at least—may recede into the background. This is not to say that all the time you've spent surfing Instagram, playing video games, or watching TV has been a waste. But generally, the digital world is more of a time sink than it is a reservoir of memories.

There are exceptions to this, of course. Not all digital activities are devoid of meaning. You may be a film buff who remembers every scene of every movie you've ever watched, or a computer programmer who writes software to help surgeons see more patients every day. You may have even met your significant other online. I personally look back fondly on the books I've written on my computer, the life-changing emails I've received, and obviously that one time Taylor Swift Liked one of my tweets. But for me, and probably for you, these are the "exceptions that prove the rule."

In addition to making us more calm and balanced, the analog world has yet another benefit as it relates to making time more memorable: it slows down our *perception* of time. This lets us process events more deeply and remember more of them as a result. In savoring the past and reminiscing about our lives, we gloss over the routine: the psychology of time tells us that the more novel our life is, the more slowly time moves. For our mind, novel events are markers in time, guideposts we can look back at to judge how far we've come. In other words, novelty is not just something we gravitate to in the moment. It's something we gravitate to when reflecting on our life—as well as a sign that a memory is worth looking back on in the first place.

While internet companies provide us with services that engage our brain's novelty bias, this novelty usually comes in the form of fleeting distraction, the digital equivalent of ropes that we hang on to as we swing over to the next one. In addition to this, novelty is relative. On the internet, because pretty much everything is novel, hardly anything is. We're walking through a digital equivalent of Times Square, so overwhelmed by stimuli that we don't process anything fully.

On the other hand, the analog world is slow, in a way that is good and meaningful. It's slow enough to process, slow enough to savor, slow enough to remember. Given we spend a ridiculous proportion of our day in front of screens, purposefully stepping back from the digital world to engage with the analog world can be considered a surefire path to calm.

Another favorite experiment from my quest for calm was devoting more time to savoring slow, quiet, analog moments. The more digital activities I replaced with analog alternatives (when substitutes were available), the more deeply I was able to experience my days. When it came time to work, I was also able to slow down enough to eschew distraction and just calmly focus on what was in front of me.

I also found that choosing analog alternatives led me to extract more meaning out of my time. While my iPad let me efficiently read research and books, I began to find far more focus in printing off studies to hunker down on them with a pen, and cracking open physical books to scribble notes in the margins. Instead of tapping around *The Economist*'s app, I subscribed to the physical edition—much like the newspaper, I found this a slower, calmer way of learning about world events, which led me to remember more. (Research suggests that the less often we fill our attention to the brim, the more we tend to remember.)

What I lost in speed, I more than made up for in focus and calm. And with no tempting distractions in sight, this had the effect of making me more efficient with how I spent my time.

Another great attribute of the analog world is how it provides us with some mental space to turn inward and process our thoughts more thoroughly. Digitally, we rarely step back to reflect, turn over ideas, or dig deep in our mind for creative solutions to problems. We're too busy swinging from one branch—an idea, a link, or a video—to the next.[*]

**Analog activities give our mind room to think.** When our mind wanders, it automatically unearths ideas, plans for the future, and recharges. Just think about your last shower—or the last time your mind had a chance to wander, a mental mode, which, when we enter it deliberately, I call "scatterfocus."[†] In showers past, you've probably pieced together solutions to problems, planned for the day ahead, and left feeling energized.

In my own quest for calm, the more digital activities I substituted for analog ones, the calmer I became. If you're looking for inspiration to lower your stimulation height through the analog world, here are some substitutions I found helpful.

- **Writing.** I'm writing these words on my computer because that's more efficient—writing this book longhand would easily take twice as long (if I could even read my scribbles later on).

---

[*] It's worth noting that at some point, the internet is likely to go from a 2D layer we interact with via a screen to a 3D layer we can overlay on top of our analog reality, a concept often called "mixed reality" or the "metaverse." Only time will tell how this future will unfold—and what it will look like. Whatever happens, this mixed reality will likely remain more dopaminergic than our analog world and will probably prove equally worth stepping back from.

[†] I should probably mention that I explore this subject in great depth in my previous book *Hyperfocus*. I personally dislike when authors promote their other books in their current one, so feel free to not buy this previous book to get back at me for this.

But with more meaningful writing—letters to friends, journaling, and mapping out my future—I'll go analog. I'm a big fan of fountain pens, which help me slow down and create a relaxing ritual around writing. (There's also something oddly calming about cleaning and refilling a fountain pen.)

- **The to-do list.** As someone who studies personal productivity for a living, I've tried out more to-do apps than I can count. Somewhere in my calm journey, I decided to delete all of my task-management apps and switch to paper, capturing my daily intentions and to-dos the analog way on a large legal pad on my desk (with my favorite TWSBI fountain pen, of course). Managing time this way is slower but more deliberate. As a general rule, the slower you plan, the more deliberately you act.

- **Time with friends.** Staying connected with friends on social media is stimulating but not all that rewarding. For this reason, I stopped counting digital social media time as time with friends. To count as friend time, we have to be together in person or communicate through a medium richer than text (phone calls count). I see friendship as the sum of the attention I share with someone. This attention is more fruitful when shared synchronously and in person.

- **Physical books.** I'm a big fan of audiobooks and e-books. But when I want to sink deeply into a good book, I'll almost always go analog. I find the physicality of the book makes the whole experience more engaging. As I've mentioned, I've started to read books for work in this way, too—so I can make notes in the margins and flip around to connect ideas with less friction.

- **Games.** A bad habit I kicked at the start of my journey to calm was playing simple, unrewarding games on my phone that were designed to be superstimulating and addictive. (If you doubt how addictive a game on your phone can be, try downloading *Subway Surfers*. Actually, don't: I've burned through more time on this game than I want to admit.) As a substitute for these digital games, I bought a bunch of board games and puzzles. The best part is that most of these games involve other people, making the activity even more meaningful.

- **Looking up words.** Whenever I came across an unfamiliar word, I began making an effort to look it up in the hardback *Oxford English Reference Dictionary* we keep in the living room. This leads me to remember the words more. After all, the book's entire surface area is devoted to them, not sidebar ads or ways to share definitions on social media (as if that's something people actually want to do). The best part: my wife and I used this dictionary as our wedding guest book, where everyone could circle words that reminded them of us. These notes make looking up words even more fun. (Or at least as fun as looking up words can be.)

- **The news.** I stopped consuming digital news entirely following my first dopamine fast, opting for two morning newspapers. A physical newspaper is my favorite subscription service: an affordable daily briefing that contains everything you need to know about what's going on in your city, country, and the world. Better yet, subscribing puts the onus on the *newspaper* to keep you informed—you don't have to navigate several websites to filter through the news for yourself. If you don't have to respond to hourly events in your work or life, consider subscribing to one. This can be an admittedly annoying tactic in an age when a lot of newspapers are ideologically entrenched and warp the day's events through a polarized lens. Again, though, as with the rest of the advice in this book, try this tactic only if you think it'll work for you. (I find that the newspapers in my city are balanced enough to make this strategy worthwhile.)

In the Venn diagram of our digital and analog lives, activities like these exist in the middle. As such, they're the low-hanging fruit that can lead us to more meaningful levels of calm. We typically don't lose any time through techniques like these—we just get things done differently and more thoughtfully.

In addition to doing more things the analog way, it's worth connecting with activities we can do *only* in the analog world.

Analog-only activities have been shown to absorb extra stress, which creates more space between us and our burnout threshold. They're less dopaminergic—they still do release dopamine, but do so while also rewarding us with a balanced blend of neurotransmitters that make us feel happy, connected, and in some cases, euphoric. If you find yourself with some extra time after weeding out dopaminergic distraction, these activities will lead you to feel rested, rejuvenated, and above all else, calm. They'll also lead you to a state of productive presence with what's in front of you.

The most helpful habits for calm have two things in common: they are not only analog, but also make our primitive brain happy. In this chapter, I'll highlight my four favorite habits, which research suggests lead us to the most significant levels of calm.

Those activities are movement, time with people, meditation, and fueling your body mindfully.

## Finding Joy in Movement

Just as we gravitate to what's instant in the digital world, we gravitate to what's convenient in the analog world. This applies to getting physical activity throughout our day. Few of us walk or bike to work, and once we're at work, many of us work with our minds rather than with our hands. On some level, we prefer this: it's less physical effort, and effort is an ingredient our body and mind prefer to conserve.

Unfortunately, this means we're mismatched to our environment: our bodies are designed to be active. We need to move our body in order to still our mind. If you find yourself squirming in your office chair after sitting for too long, experience the inexplicable urge to get up throughout the day, or often feel physically restless, this might just be why. Historically, we evolved to walk between 8 and 14.5 kilometers (5 and 9 miles) daily. Now we get around five thousand steps a day—just 4 kilometers (2.5 miles). Our ancestors would have had to *try* to get this little activity.

A standard recommendation is that we should aim for ten thousand steps a day. When we dig deeper into the source for this number, though, it quickly starts to feel arbitrary. One study found that the number's origins "can be traced to Japanese walking clubs and a business slogan [from] 30+ years ago." While the number is an easy recommendation to make, ten thousand steps clocks in at a little over 8 kilometers (5 miles). That *just* gets you to a level of physical activity that your body is designed for. On top of this, you might find it a chore to fit so many steps into your life. At least I did, as someone who works from home.

This recommendation also doesn't account for the wondrous array of movement options available to us, many of which are infinitely more fun than going on a daily constitutional walk. A yoga workout might provide you with only a handful of steps, but it will still leave your body feeling nice and balanced after. Go for a one-hour swim, and you'd be lucky to register even a few steps on your fitness tracker—but your body and mind will see things differently. Vigorously doing chores around the house—working up a sweat scrubbing the floors, wiping down the kitchen cabinets, and dusting the bookshelves—isn't usually viewed as exercise, but it gets your heart rate up just the same.

Here's a rule worth living by: get at least 150 minutes of moderate activity or 75 minutes of vigorous exercise every week—the United States Department of Health and Human Services' weekly recommendation for regular physical activity. And while you do, keep in mind that this is the bare minimum to get you moving. Daily, this means getting *at least* 20 minutes of light activity (equivalent to a brisk walk or a swim), or 10 minutes of vigorous exercise (running, cycling, kickboxing, breakdancing, or anything else that works up a good sweat). Once you move a little, chances are you'll want to keep going—especially when you move in ways that you love. Use these numbers as a starting point—the level of physical activity you won't go below.

To help write this section, I asked Kelly McGonigal, a lecturer at Stanford University and the author of *The Joy of Movement* and *The Willpower Instinct*, if she had any recommendations for someone looking to move according to how we're wired. She's a firm believer that if you feel as though you just don't like exercise, you haven't found the correct dose, type, or community that "would transform you into an exercise person." There are countless options available: she's a fan of group dance classes, kickboxing, lifting weights, and high-intensity interval training. During the project, I began to love indoor cycling classes, throwing a Frisbee around in the park, and doing yoga workouts on YouTube. Every day, I tried to double the bare minimum.

Variety is key. Experiment with as many different types of movement as you can to find one or two that stick. Blow the dust off the trampoline in the basement, join a dance class, or treat yourself to time on social media—but only after you spend an equivalent amount of time running. Instead of drinking your morning cup of coffee in front of the computer, walk to your favorite café or to a nearby green space to savor the drink outside. Go fly a (literal) kite, set a maximum for how much time you'll sit every day, or go on outdoor outings with your friends or family—hiking, biking, and walking around downtown all work well for this. Volunteer in ways that will make you active, incorporate stretching into your routine by making it a part of your post-work wind-down ritual, conduct more walking meetings, or do more gardening out in your backyard or a community space. Try moving in as many ways as you can. Keep what you love, even if those activities take a while to find.

In the process of finding an exercise that fits, be mindful of any negative self-talk that arises. It's almost sure to come up—and when it does, try to register that it has, while also questioning its validity. Our mind tends to turn to the negative when we think about exercise—especially given so many of us work out because we want to change the way we look, not because we love our bodies and want to reward them with energizing movement. A negative inner dialogue around exercise is usually untrue and prevents us from working toward our goals and enjoying ourselves along the way.

As McGonigal said to me, "So many of people's negative experiences with movement come from the way fitness and exercise are often framed as ways to make your body more acceptable." Move because moving feels good—and because you'll feel amazing after.

On top of trying out a variety of exercises to see what sticks, McGonigal has two other recommendations to get even more out of our active time: experiment with group exercise if you can, and spend some time in nature. Group exercise can provide you with community and connect you with others. This releases oxytocin, while letting you feel connected to others while exercising. As McGonigal put it, "When you move in synchronicity with other people, it bonds you. It releases endorphins that relieve pain, and boosts your mood as you move with others." Studies show that we experience these benefits regardless of whether we're moving in sync with other people in the analog world, or in the digital world through a live Zoom workout.

We evolved to thrive surrounded by nature, not in concrete environments dotted and edged with trees and shrubs. Time in nature also calms you with no additional effort required on your part. McGonigal's research suggests that outdoor exercise can also lead to profound mental health benefits and even help with more significant struggles such as "suicidal thinking, depression, trauma, and grief."

The bottom line: however you can, however feels good to you, move. Remember the lesson from McGonigal's research: if you think exercise isn't for you, you probably just haven't found a fun way of moving that fits with who you are.

## People Time

If you want to go fast, go alone. If you want to go far, go together.

PROVERB (ORIGIN UNKNOWN)

Everyone's pandemic story is different, but something that many have in common is the fact that, while our screen time went up, we spent less time in the presence of other people.

As with movement, spending time with others gives us more than just an energy boost. We *need* to spend time with others, in person—our bodies and minds depend on it. One recent study found that loneliness is as damaging to our overall health as *smoking fifteen cigarettes every day*. (Smoking is the leading cause of preventable death in the United States.) This same study found that loneliness can prove riskier to our longevity than being physically inactive. Yet another study found that the strength of our social circles is "a better predictor of self-reported stress, happiness and well-being levels than fitness tracker data on physical activity, heart rate and sleep."

My favorite meta-analysis on the topic summed up the results of studies that had a combined total of more than three million participants, to "establish the overall and relative magnitude of social isolation and loneliness." What they found was staggering: social isolation, loneliness, and living alone increase our odds of early death by around *25 to 30 percent*.

Time with other people doesn't just keep our minds chemically balanced and calm. It leads us to a longer and healthier life, extending our life span and *health* span.

Our mind deeply desires connection with other people. We make this time back—not just in calm productivity, but also in a longer life.

Early on in my journey to calm, I found that I had to come to terms with an uncomfortable truth: that I had few deep personal friendships, and that my mental health suffered for it. As a more introverted person, I would tell myself that I'd rather hunker down with a good book than spend time with others. Digging deeper, I found that this storytelling was a defense mechanism: I was hiding from myself the fact that I felt anxious in social situations, and as a result, kept people at arm's length.

While I had developed dozens of loose friendships, I had few deeper ones (setting aside the bonds I had with my wife and immediate family).

Noticing this, I made a focused effort to up the level of social inter-action in my life. After lowering my height of stimulation, this became easier: I started to *crave* face time with other people. So I started to ex-periment to see what stuck.

I tried a lot of things on for size, and a lot didn't work. Around Christmastime, attending a local hockey game with my wife and a friend, I walked by a men's barbershop chorus. They sounded heavenly. One of the performers saw that I was enjoying the music, and handed me his business card, in case I was curious about joining the group. I joined, but bailed after attending a few rehearsals, after finding out how seriously some folks in the group took things. (Note to self: next time join a singing group that *doesn't* compete in national competi-tions.) I tried taking a local improv class, with the hopes of finding a few fellow free-spirited folks to hang out with. This was fun, but I didn't connect with the group as much as I thought I would. I made plans to join a Friday night knitting group—even though I'm a relative newbie—but the knitting shop closed down as I was about to join. (I find that knitting leads me to come up with a ton of new ideas. It's eas-ily one of the most underrated productivity habits.)

Luckily, other endeavors proved more fruitful. I began seeing a therapist, who made me aware of my social anxiety in the first place and let me talk through what made me uncomfortable. While this didn't lead me to calm directly, it helped me overcome mental road-blocks for spending time with others. I teamed up with a few work friends to form a work accountability group, to meet every week to talk about strategy and our personal goals. This let me invest in a few bud-ding friendships, while counterbalancing the lack of connection in my work that had led me to burn out. I blocked out more time for the friendships I already had in my life so that I could deepen them: old friends from high school, friends I volunteered with every summer, and friends I knew around town. I made an effort to work one or two social things into my calendar every week. When traveling for work, I would also think about whether I knew anyone in the cities I traveled to, to see if they had time to grab dinner or tea.

This newfound social interaction didn't just make me feel more calm and balanced. It filled me with more energy as these connections and friendships deepened.

The most bountiful wellspring of calm in the analog world is easily human connection.

I should say with full disclosure that more than any other idea in this book, connecting with other people is the strategy I'm continuing to work on the most. Generally speaking, I've found that three rules are worth following when it comes to time with others:

1. **Digital socialization doesn't count.** Internalize this rule: time spent socializing in the digital world doesn't count as social time. Your mind just doesn't view it the same way: digital connection is simulated, and if you can't reach out and touch someone, it doesn't count. Analog socialization takes more effort but provides us with more calm.

2. **Experiment, experiment, experiment.** As with exercise, it might take you a few tries to find ideal ways of spending time with other people. Join a choir, take an improv class, and reconnect with people who are engaging enough that they make you forget about your phone. Keep trying things out, and keep what you like. It may take you a few tries, and that's okay. It might also take more work than you'd expect, and that's okay, too.

3. **Prioritize settling your mind.** If you're socially anxious like me, you can do this by making a deliberate effort to lower

your stimulation height. Time with people exists at a low stimulation height, and so you'll feel more comfortable socializing when you make an effort to settle your mind at the same time. Plus, as a bonus, you'll feel the compulsion to pick up your phone less often. Your time will also feel more memorable and enjoyable, not to mention less fragmented.

If you have found that your time with others has gone down as your time with technology has gone up, experiment as soon as you can to find ways of upping the level of social interaction in your life. This effort is always worthwhile, because of our biological need to feel connected with others. Even if you're an introvert, you need genuine human connection just the same.

The opportunities for more social interaction are endless. Having an "analog night" with your family is another fun tactic. The definition is in the name: for a whole evening, everyone powers down their devices to actually spend quality time, and quality attention, with one another. The artificial sense of community provided by social media is no match for this deep, face-to-face, personal connection.

One additional strategy worth mentioning is to focus also on *helping* others. When caring for others feels like a stressful obligation, it drains us. But when we care for others in situations where we can do three things—practice empathy, act autonomously, and connect with *why* we're helping—that time refuels us. While anxiety is an emotion that tends to draw us inward, when we turn outward and toward other people, we feel energized, relaxed, while full of life. As Stanford professor Jamil Zaki wrote in *The Atlantic*, "people are psychologically intertwined, such that helping others is a kindness to ourselves" in the same way that "watching over ourselves supports others." He recommends the strategy of having an "other-care" day instead of a *self*-care day—an approach worth trying out if you're looking to experiment with methods of connection.

When we deprive our brains of the opportunity to be social, we become more anxious. We thrive and find calm when surrounded by people—not screens.

## Practicing Presence

When I asked Dan Lieberman, coauthor of the book *The Molecule of More*, what the easiest way of engaging our brain's here-and-now network is, he gave me an easy one-word answer: meditation.

If you've read any of my previous work, you'll know that I'm a big fan of meditation. I'm even a fan of meditating for productivity reasons, in part because the practice leads us to become resilient against distraction. Meditation also lowers our overall stimulation height, which allows us to focus more easily. For every minute we spend meditating, we make back even more in what we're able to get done. It's for these reasons that I think everyone should try out the practice—even (or perhaps especially) if the mere thought of meditation puts you off or feels hippie-dippie to you on the surface.

Luckily, meditation is far more straightforward than you'd expect. Here's how to meditate, in just two bullet points:

- Sit down with your back straight and your eyes closed, and bring your full attention to the details of your breath. Notice all you can about it, including its flow, temperature, and how it moves in and out of your body.
- When your mind wanders—and it will, often—once again draw your attention back to your breath.

That's it! Try not to overthink the practice: it doesn't matter what you do with your hands, whether you're sitting in a chair or on a meditation cushion, and you can even choose to keep your eyes open, if your environment isn't full of distracting visual cues.

Meditation is simple—so much so that at first you'll probably think you're doing it wrong. But this simplicity is precisely what makes the practice so powerful.

While meditation is easy in theory, you'll find that your mind will put up a fight when you give it a shot. The practice may feel impossible—so impossible that you'll put it off, even when you set aside time for the ritual in advance.

But that is precisely the point of meditation. If you can find calm while focusing on your breath—when your mind is putting up a hell of a fight to focus on something so simple—it will become infinitely easier to find calm the rest of the day, too. This is especially true when your self-talk runs rampant, or when your external world is noisy. A truth about meditation is that if you keep calm while focusing on your breath, you can stay calm doing pretty much anything. It's hard to imagine an activity that lives at a lower stimulation height. For this reason, if you can learn to *engage* with your breath, you can become engaged with pretty much anything.

Meditation is also great because it's an opportunity to notice which anxiety-fueled thoughts tug at your attention throughout the day. Again, your mind will constantly wander during meditation, and that's okay. The point is to notice when it does, and gently draw your attention back to your breath—maybe after laughing about how stubborn your mind can be. Expect your mind to wander, and return to your breath when it does.

Contrary to what some believe, the purpose of meditation is not to stop your mind from thinking. This is impossible: your mind will constantly generate thoughts (if it stops doing so, you have bigger problems). It could even be said that our mind *compulsively* generates thoughts in response to what happens around us.

The thoughts our mind generates can fuel the cycle of anxiety—but meditation helps us notice this tendency of our mind. The act of noticing that our mind has wandered, and then welcoming our attention back to our breath, lets us create a small but meaningful amount of distance between our thoughts. Noticing our wandering mind, we intentionally reorient our thinking toward our breath. This provides us with the space we need to step back from what we're thinking, evaluate our thoughts, think about whether they're true, and, one breath after the next, gain slightly more control over our attention.

As we learn to step back from the narratives we construct about our lives, we can notice which stories are true, and which thoughts are driven by cycles of anxiety. Over time, we generate fewer untrue thoughts, and become immersed in the present.

In doing so, we discover greater depths of calm.

Of course, meditation also unleashes many neurochemicals that settle our mind. I personally find the calm feeling that meditation provides to be a stronger motivator than factually understanding which calm chemicals the practice leads our brain to release. But, if you're looking to boost chemicals of calm, you can rest (and breathe) easy. At once, meditation unleashes serotonin on our mind, increasing our happiness, while melting away cortisol. One study found that meditation can release as many endorphins as a run. Forget a runner's high—how about a meditation high?

Meditation is not easy. It's also not fun, at least at first. Your mind will try to justify why you shouldn't spend time on the practice. But the more you can overcome your thoughts to focus on your breath—and to meditate in the first place—the calmer your mind will become.

Once meditation becomes a part of your daily life, thoughts will get in your way far less often—and you'll even become more productive to boot.

While this book focuses on deeper changes to find calm, it is also possible to use breathing exercises as a way to find calm in the more *immediate* term. This can be especially helpful for coping with periods of high *acute* stress. One way to do this is through stimulating our body's vagus nerve. This nerve is a core component of our parasympathetic nervous system, the part of our nervous system that's active when we're relaxed and not stressed. This nerve also connects the body to the brain. By stimulating this nerve, we find greater calm.*

Two surefire ways of stimulating this nerve are yawning and slow breathing. Slow breathing works especially well when we breathe from our belly and exhale for longer than we inhale.

Another non-breath way to stimulate the vagus nerve is to soften your gaze so that your eyes aren't focused on anything in particular. If you find it tough to wrap your head around this idea, think about how your eyes soften and relax when taking in a sweeping panorama—when looking out at the ocean, the stars, or at a sunset.

It's even possible to combine all of these techniques to find calm very quickly. Set a timer for five minutes, yawn a time or two, and then practice four-eight breathing—breathing in for four seconds and out for eight—while softening your eyes. Try not to pay attention to anything besides your breath until the timer runs out. If your mind grows impatient—or rather *when* your mind grows impatient—just bring it

---

* The other part of our body's autonomic nervous system, the sympathetic nervous system, activates when we experience stressful events. It's what is responsible for our fight-flight-freeze response.

back to your breath. This activity will allow you to experience the benefits of meditation, while producing physical changes in your body that lead you to greater depths of calm—in just five minutes. If you find all of this too much to tackle at once, choose one or two of these techniques to try out. They're all quick shortcuts to finding calm in a stressful situation.

## Caffeine and Calm

In addition to movement, people, and meditation, the more we consume food that our body is built to thrive on, the calmer—and more energized!—we feel. We'll talk about actual food in a bit—but first, let's cover caffeine.

To see how caffeine affected my sense of calm, midway through the project I decided to conduct another experiment to reset my tolerance to the drug.

Before the experiment, I had grown to love my morning ritual of thoughtfully preparing a bowl of matcha tea. On quieter mornings, crawling out of bed, I'd mosey on over to the kitchen to heat some water to a precise 80 degrees Celsius. The ritual was a calm one to wake up to: sifting the matcha powder in the bowl so that it became fine dust, whisking that powder with a wee bit of hot water to make the matcha concentrate, and finally whisking that with more water to finish off the delicious, frothy bowl. On days when I needed even more energy, I loved my AeroPress coffee ritual just the same, but I won't go into that, because then you might put down this book and never finish it. Both items were on my savor list, but in a weird way, I was excited to see what would happen if I gave them up for a bit.

I decided to just rip the proverbial bandage off and go cold turkey.

On the first day, I was surprised by how little withdrawal I felt (I had four cups of coffee the previous day as a sort of last hurrah). Apart from a slight headache before bed, I felt pretty great, and got a surprising amount of work done on a day I thought I wouldn't have been able to.

The second day was when the withdrawal symptoms hit me like a six-ton tractor-trailer. The effects were so bad that I had to lie down in bed for some of the day. Leading up to the experiment, the amount of caffeine in my diet had risen to the equivalent of two or three small cups of coffee a day. But this experiment made it quickly evident that I had grown dependent on the drug. On day two, I felt like I had come down with the flu—I got far less done and had little energy for hobbies, and my wife became concerned that I actually was sick. As she joked to me, "I don't know whether to treat you as if you have the flu or you're just recovering from a chemical dependency." (It was the latter.)

Luckily, the roughest withdrawal symptoms tapered off quite a bit on day three. That morning, I popped an Advil, which cut my headache, and felt mostly fine, even if I still dragged my feet somewhat to get stuff done. I had slightly less motivation than usual, but with a couple of projects on tight deadlines, I didn't feel the dip as much as I would have otherwise.

The symptoms would continue to taper off until around the ninth day. I found that exercising more, getting more rest, taking the occasional Advil to combat the headaches, and drinking more water helped immensely with the symptoms.

Ten days in, my energy rose to a level equivalent to the amount I had while regularly consuming caffeine. Most of us view caffeine as a stimulant, but the truth is that our body adjusts to how much caffeine we consume, until the caffeine no longer makes a difference. When we habitually consume a certain amount of caffeine, we need to continue consuming at that same amount to feel like ourselves again.

As I adjusted downward, I felt calmer. A lot calmer. Not only did I sleep better without caffeine—which in itself led me to energy, balance, and calm—my days became more effortless, too. (Sleep is yet another analog element of our lives we should be doubling down on in our pursuit of calm. If you're consistently getting fewer than the recommended seven and a half to eight hours, invest in a nighttime ritual that gets you to bed on time, or a calming morning routine that you look forward to each day. A lack of sleep is a common trigger for episodes of anxiety, which makes investing in sleep hygiene even more important.)

Finding calm at the end of the reset, my mind didn't put up a fight to finish small tasks. I felt less guilty about taking breaks from work, because my mind was more settled. And I craved distraction less, too. Caffeine stimulates the release of dopamine, which can lead us to engage in additional dopaminergic behavior. (If you're curious to test this out, try consuming more caffeine than usual, and see if you crave more distraction at the higher stimulation height.)

A week and a half into the reset, at around 9:00 p.m., I found myself worried, though. I had an unusually high amount of energy for that time of day, which, before the reset, meant I would struggle to fall asleep. Before the experiment, I had felt this energized before bed only on days when I consumed a lot of caffeine. Of course, on this day, I had a different energy source: I wasn't stressing my body and wasn't alternating between energy spikes and slumps, my energy spiking with caffeine and plummeting as the caffeine left my system. My energy was consistent, strong, and lasting. And even though it was high at the end of the day, that didn't matter much.

My concern was misplaced: I fell asleep within a few minutes of lying down.

Caffeine has become an integral part of our days and our lives—but it's also a drug that we can grow to depend on. If you don't like the thought of giving it up because of the symptoms you'll experience (including reduced energy in the short term), you've likely grown dependent on the drug, too.

That is okay, and obviously I'm not going to tell you what you should and shouldn't eat and drink. But caffeine is an interesting thing to turn our attention to in order to examine how what we eat and drink influences how calm we feel. Generally speaking, food affects our neurochemistry more than we think.

We often think of caffeine as liquid energy, but a better analogy is liquid stress, or even liquid adrenaline. As we consume caffeine, our body has little choice but to boost how much adrenaline and cortisol it produces. Caffeine has been shown to increase cortisol production, as well as the production of the stress hormone epinephrine, also known as adrenaline, by around *200 percent*. This holds true even after our body adjusts to how much we consume. We're highly alert, but only because caffeine leads our body to release these stress hormones, which mobilize us to get stuff done. Given that chronic stress and anxiety already lead to elevated levels of these hormones, consuming caffeine can make us unbearably anxious.

Caffeine doesn't feel stressful to drink—and that's because, along with adrenaline and cortisol, the drug leads to the aforementioned rush of dopamine (stimulation) and also serotonin (happiness). We feel happy and stimulated, which reinforces the caffeine habit—and makes conducting a caffeine detox more difficult, because withdrawing from consumption leads our mood to dip in the absence of these chemicals.

It's worth noting that caffeine affects everyone differently. Not only have most of us adjusted to different levels of the drug, but our physiology responds differently, too. Some of us are jittery after a few sips, while others can pound back one cup after another, barely feeling a thing. Regardless of your consumption level, if you feel anxious, it may be worth cutting back. I found this firsthand after doing the reset.

With fewer stress hormones coursing through my body and mind, I found that resetting my caffeine tolerance—while a pain for a few days—proved immensely helpful in my journey to calm. I'm more sensitive to caffeine than most, so your mileage may vary with this strategy. But once I had made my way through the initial energy dip, I found myself less anxious, and noticed that my thoughts rolled over onto themselves far less often. My mental energy felt cleaner burning; my mind became clearer, my productivity more consistent, my energy lasting late into the evening, long after it would have dipped from the usual midafternoon caffeine crash. And I moved closer to calm.

If you feel anxious, moody, or nervous after consuming caffeine, I recommend a caffeine reset. This may be the most painful thing I ask you to do in this book, second to the dopamine fast, but I think you'll find the experiment very worthwhile. The benefits can be profound. Caffeine consumption has long been linked to anxiety and panic attacks—there is even a diagnosis in the *DSM-5*, the manual for psychiatric diagnoses in the United States, named *caffeine-induced anxiety disorder*. Given that the substance affects everyone differently, it may be affecting you more than you think.

If you face a lot of untamable chronic stress, caffeine shouldn't be another source you add to the pile.

Here are a few tips if you do decide to reset your caffeine tolerance:

- **Try doing the reset the next time you come down with the flu or a cold.** This way, your mind will attribute withdrawal symptoms, many of which are flulike (chills, weakness, and lethargy) to the fact that you're sick, not the fact that you're weaning yourself off a drug. Also, try starting the reset on the weekend or a Friday so you can relax a bit during the initial energy dip.

- **You can either go cold turkey, or gradually reduce how much caffeine you consume every day.** Going cold turkey is straightforward enough: just go from drinking your regular amount of caffeine to none. You can also gradually reduce how much you consume, by slowly substituting more and more of your caffeinated coffee or tea with decaf options.

- **Be sure to cultivate your energy levels during the reset, particularly during the first week, by upping how much exercise, rest, water, and sleep you get.** This will help compensate for the dip from the lack of caffeine. Or, if you're curious, stick with your daily routines, to notice just how dependent you've gotten on the drug.

- **Watch out for *hidden* sources of caffeine.** There is caffeine lurking in most soft drinks: a twelve-ounce can of Diet Coke contains forty-six milligrams of caffeine, as much as some shots of espresso. There's also caffeine lurking in decaffeinated coffee—a decaf coffee at Starbucks, for example, can contain as much as thirty milligrams of the drug. If you do opt for decaf coffee, check that it's decaffeinated using the Swiss Water method, which cuts out nearly all of the stimulant.

- **If you're struggling with the reset, increase how many caffeinated beverages you consume that contain L-theanine.** L-theanine is an amino acid found in green tea (and matcha) that significantly reduces how much adrenaline your body produces in response to caffeine. As a result, you experience less of a stress response. L-theanine has also been shown to boost focus while lowering how anxious you feel. Green tea is my favorite caffeine delivery mechanism for this reason. L-theanine in green tea also leads to a slight dopamine release—and this holds true *regardless of whether the green tea is caffeinated*. This generally makes green tea an excellent substitute for coffee: you still get the benefits of consuming caffeine, but without the extreme stress response.

At its best, caffeine fires us up, makes us happy, and narrows our attention so we can focus on one thing. At its worst, caffeine makes us anxious and adds unnecessary stress to our lives, usually without our realizing it. Conducting a reset may help you discover which camp you fall in to.

If you don't find that you feel calm after the experiment, do feel free to go back. But if you're anything like me (and so many others), you might be surprised by both the energy you have and the depths of calm you reach.

## Hangxiety

Speaking of beverages with drugs in them: consuming alcohol also upsets our neurochemistry. Alcohol is a drug that is consumed often—and often to excess. In one recent survey from 2019 conducted by the National Institute on Alcohol Abuse and Alcoholism (NIAAA), around 54.9 percent of Americans over eighteen have had a drink in the last month. While that isn't that high a dose, 25.8 percent of those over eighteen have also engaged in *binge drinking* in the past month.* Surprisingly, alcohol consumption is one of the leading preventable causes of death in the US, after smoking tobacco, a poor diet, and not enough physical activity.

Up until a few years ago, I counted myself in the group of those who drank to excess. While I didn't drink alcohol more than a couple of times a week, when I had a drink, I usually ended up having two. When I had two, I typically had three. And when I had three . . . you get the idea. For me, drinking alcohol has always been a slippery slope, a distraction that temporarily hid problems and stress from my view. The morning after drinking episodes, though, a bit hungover, I'd often wake up feeling anxious, filled with dread. This post-boozing phenomenon is popular enough to have a slang name: hangxiety.

As George F. Koob, the director of the NIAAA, succinctly summed it up, "I think of a hangover as, more or less, a mini-withdrawal from alcohol, and *anxiety is one of the components*" (emphasis mine).

This makes sense when you examine the ways alcohol affects our

---

* Binge drinking is defined as a pattern of drinking enough to bring the blood alcohol content to 0.08 g/dL or higher. According to the NIAAA, this usually happens "after a woman consumes 4 or more drinks or a man consumes 5 or more drinks—in about 2 hours."

brain: research shows that alcohol affects the production of a bunch of neurochemicals at once. Alcohol makes us feel three things as we consume it: thrilled, happy, and relaxed. These are great feelings! But there's a catch: we experience a brutal comedown from them all.

First, alcohol leads our brain to produce more dopamine, which provides us with a rush. It's no wonder we want another drink so quickly after the first. Critically, though, the alcohol withdrawal that follows then leads to a *decrease* in dopamine production. Serotonin is also produced when we consume alcohol—this is why drinking alcohol can feel good when we're still experiencing the effects of the drug. Unfortunately, serotonin production is suppressed during the withdrawal stage (at least in one study conducted on rats). Alcohol also affects GABA levels in our brain. GABA is a neurochemical that leads us to feel relaxed— many of the activities in this chapter also lead to a GABA release. But while mild amounts of alcohol increase GABA activity, more significant amounts sadly temporarily *deplete* GABA in our brain. This makes us feel less relaxed, more tense, and often panicked.

Consuming alcohol would be more of a no-brainer if there were no comedown. Unfortunately, what starts as a happy yet relaxed thrill invariably ends in withdrawal—not to mention a comedown from all three effects. If you find, as I did, that alcohol makes your anxiety worse— including the morning after—it may be worth cutting back on the drug or eliminating it entirely. (And do seek medical help if you find that you are dependent on the drug and experience severe withdrawal symptoms.)

These days, my alcohol consumption rule is simple: only consume the drug when the drink itself is novel (e.g., a tumbler of fancy scotch or some exciting-sounding specialty drink at a restaurant), or when doing so is part of a fun ritual (e.g., going on a family wine tour or celebrating one of my wife's accomplishments).

In the moment, having a few drinks can lead you to feel happy, relaxed, and energized. In practice, though, consuming alcohol can prove nothing more than a way of borrowing happiness, energy, and calm from the following morning.

## Eating Your Way to Calm

Here's the challenge with writing a book about a subject as expansive as calm: when you zoom out far enough, pretty much everything we do influences how calm we feel. That's why this particular chapter is one of the longest ones in the book. Every single activity we engage with releases a different concoction of neurochemicals. In addition to the factors of calm I've mentioned so far—spending more time in the analog world, getting your body moving, spending time with people, meditating, and establishing a healthier relationship with caffeine and alcohol—let's zero in on one more. The final factor worth covering is the food we eat.

As it relates to food, stress does two things to our body. **At once, stress causes us to eat more, while tempting us to eat less healthfully**. By taming sources of chronic stress—and investing in calming strategies to deal with our remaining sources—we don't just become more engaged and less likely to burn out. We also hold on to less body fat.

If you're curious, here's the mechanism through which your body retains fat in response to stressful situations. First, you encounter a stressful event, which floods your body with cortisol, the stress hormone. This flood of cortisol leads your body to release a surge of glucose (energy) so that your body has the resources to face down the source of stress.

In most of human history, we made good use of this glucose! We had a real, genuine threat to fight or flee, and weren't just sitting down releasing cortisol in response to some tweet. Our body used up the glucose that stress provided us with.

Today, as chronic stress builds up inside of us like a pressurized drum, our blood glucose level rises in turn. Once we don't make use of this glucose, our blood sugar levels rise, and so too does our insulin level—insulin is the hormone that lets us convert glucose into energy that our body believes it needs. With higher blood sugar and insulin levels, our body then secretes a hunger hormone called ghrelin, which leads us to eat more and gain weight.

Stress sets off a chain reaction; it's the first domino in a lineup of several that leads us to eat more and store more body fat. Over time, chronically elevated levels of stress—and glucose and insulin—not only lead us to gain weight, but also can lead us to develop diabetes and insulin resistance. Anxiety, depression, and insomnia have all been correlated with excess insulin production.

If you have some stubborn body fat that won't go away, no matter how well you eat or how much you exercise, especially if that fat is around your midsection, chronic stress may be the problem.*

Either way, even if you eat less during stressful times, what you eat probably does change. During periods of high stress, we have been shown to eat more comfort foods—chocolate, savory snacks, and baked goods included—and fewer healthful foods, like fruits, vegetables, and unprocessed meats. And when we feel sad at the same time that we feel stressed, we tend to eat fattier and sweeter foods that researchers label as "hedonically rewarding."

This can lead to a stress cycle, especially given refined sugar, low-fiber

---

* Curiously, not all of us eat more in response to stress. During stressful periods, 40 percent of us tend to eat more, 20 percent eat about the same amount, and 40 percent eat less. Those who have a bit of extra weight to begin with are likelier to eat more—perhaps because belly fat *itself* has been found to secrete stress hormones.

foods, and refined grains all elevate our cortisol levels, much as caffeine does.

Luckily for us, this stress-food relationship is a two-way street. Stress influences what and how much we eat—but **what we eat also influences how stressed out we feel**.

It's possible to eat in a way that leads our body to become less stressed. Complex carbohydrates—whole grains, fruits, vegetables, nuts, seeds, and legumes—all actively lower our cortisol levels, while leading us to produce more serotonin, the happiness molecule. According to Henry Emmons, the author of *The Chemistry of Calm*, sugar and refined carbohydrates, in addition to causing the release of cortisol, can also lead to a vicious cycle, by straining "both the hormones involved and the cells' capacity to process sugar [which] further erodes the ability to produce energy, and signals the adrenals to keep the stress hormones coming."

What does all of this mean? Essentially, the food that is good for our stress levels has one thing in common: it's nutritional food that isn't mass produced or highly processed in a factory. We digest the complex carbohydrates mentioned above more slowly, and our blood doesn't get flooded with glucose all at once. We achieve greater calm by eating stuff that grows from the ground—just as our ancestors did two hundred thousand years ago.

If you find yourself craving a lot of processed food, this could be a telltale sign you still have some chronic stress left to tame.

## Keeping What Works

When we live and act in accordance with our biology, we begin to feel calmer. Living in a way that is congruent with how we're programmed to thrive can mean a lot of things, including turning away from digital superstimuli, working more movement into our days, spending time with people who energize us, practicing meditation, and consuming slower-burning foods that provide our body with lasting energy over time.

I've mentioned a lot of ideas in this chapter, and if you were to try to make all of these changes at once, you might end up biting off more than you can chew. Just start with a small, easy change or two—maybe the one or two you're most excited to make. Then, once you notice which habits stick and lead you to calm, build on those and throw out any that don't work for you.

The techniques that work best for you might come as a surprise—at least they did for me. I made some of my most meaningful strides toward calm when I started to eat less processed food. As an ardent consumer of delicious takeout food, the extent to which healthier food influenced my own feelings of calm was both a surprise and a wake-up call. For more of my life than I can remember, eating has been both a favorite pastime during the best of times, and an escape hatch I could climb down to numb any feelings of anxiety during the worst of times. Most of us have these "escape hatches" we use to avoid uncomfortable feelings. But these escape hatches are just sources of self-imposed stress that take our minds off the *other* sources of stress we face. Escape hatches vary, but can include overeating (historically my go-to), impulsive shopping, drug use (including alcohol, cannabis, and even caffeine), playing video games (including simple games like *Subway Surfers*), or turning to digital distractions like the news or social media, to swap one form of stress for another.

Some activities like these can be a source of fun and entertainment, including when we indulge intentionally. It's also okay to have a "dopamine night" every once in a while, where you engage in your favorite dopaminergic habits. But when we use these habits to escape the stress and negative emotions we face, we need to remember that our stress will be awaiting us on the other side of indulgence. And in the meantime, these escape hatches can even *add* to the stress we face.

If you find that you unintentionally indulge often, bring awareness to what triggers your impulses. Cues can include the presence of certain people, particular emotions (like boredom, loneliness, or envy), or the time of day or a preceding behavior. For me, mindless overeating almost always happened when I was stressed by something work related—which led me to both crave more unhealthy food and try to escape by eating. Also mind the stories you tell yourself throughout this process, and be sure to question any that are unkind or potentially untrue.

If you put a delicate crystal glass in the freezer for a week and then pour piping hot water into it, it's likely to shatter. The same holds true for alternating between periods of intense stress and intense indulgence.

Luckily, as you invest in the strategies in this chapter, you'll begin to notice your energy steadily increase. A couple of these habits may even serve as "keystone habits" for you. A keystone habit is the first domino in a chain that tips over a bunch of others. For example, I find meditation to be a shortcut for lowering my stimulation height, which leads me to distract myself less, giving me more time to work out and read, making me feel even calmer. You may find a similar thing with habits like cardio workouts, reading nonfiction books, drinking green tea instead of coffee, or having a consistent bedtime ritual.

Our habits never exist in isolation: they're all interconnected.

Pay attention to the habits that lead you to calm, the analog activities you're wired for that you've forgotten about as you've spent more time in the digital world. You need more of these in your life.

As we'll explore in the next chapter, you'll also earn pretty much all this time back.

## CHAPTER EIGHT

## *Calm and Productive*

The mark of a successful man is one that has spent an entire day
on the bank of a river without feeling guilty about it.

ANONYMOUS

## IKEA Chairs

If I had to name one thing I uniquely enjoy doing that other people
can't stand (after reading academic journal articles), I'd pick assembling
IKEA furniture. To me, the process of putting together anything made
by the Swedish company is immensely gratifying; there's just some-
thing about methodically following the instructions and witnessing a
dresser or cabinet come into being before your very eyes that's so satis-
fying to me. The process is simple, requires not much thinking, and yet
at the end, you're left with something you can see, hold, and use. The
feedback is immediate—the closer you are to finishing, the more as-
sembled the piece will look. And unlike with my day job, the work is
also highly tactile (mechanical keyboards aside).

As luck would have it, shortly before embarking on the journey
that became this book, my wife and I ordered some kitchen chairs from
IKEA.

Unfortunately for me, these chairs arrived in the middle of the week, and I had to leave on the weekend for some work travel. As the chief furniture assembler (CFA) of the household, unable to resist the double allure of having new chairs and assembling new IKEA stuff, I decided to put them together just after lunch. I had a light afternoon and had gotten a good amount done that morning. Plus, I figured the whole process would take no more than a couple of hours, and that the activity might be a fun way to break up the day while letting me scatter my attention.

I was right about one thing: assembling the chairs took just a couple hours. But I completely missed the mark on how enjoyable they would be to set up. Don't get me wrong: the actual assembly was as satisfying as usual. What I didn't anticipate going into the activity was what would happen in my mind, the sheer amount of guilt that would arise from stepping back from my work.

Almost immediately after sitting down next to the six boxes, I began considering the opportunity cost of my time, thinking about all the "better" things I could be doing instead. I had articles I could be writing, talks I could be prepping for, and consulting clients I could be helping. On top of this, the guilt of stepping back from superstimuli felt real and palpable. Email was piling up, social media messages were going unanswered, and there were business metrics I hadn't checked up on. Not only did I feel anxious and restless, in the moment, I felt like I was working on the exact wrong thing, which flooded my mind with doubt and negative self-talk.

A few things stick out to me as I look back at this simple little episode of guilt. The first is the discomfort I felt while doing the activity, which existed at a lower stimulation height than the rest of my day. Another was the guilt of disengaging from the accomplishment mindset: I would have enjoyed assembling the chairs quite a bit more if I had done so on the weekend or outside of my productive hours. Same task, different perspective.

I also couldn't become present with the activity, which prevented me from recharging. I also recall all of the mistakes I made—in one case to all six chairs, which required me to go back several steps, making the whole process take longer.

The task took longer than it should have because of how little I stepped back to invest in calm at the time. Anxiety compromised my attention, focus, and enjoyment of the project, while burnout likely played a role in why I couldn't engage with the activity. My productivity was capped, unnecessarily, by my anxious mind.

## Less Productivity

Let's nerd out for a bit to explore an idea that I personally find fascinating, and which might also give you some peace of mind as you invest in calm: how investing in calm makes us more productive.

The best productivity advice really does allow us to both earn back time and accomplish more of what we want to do. But it often misses a crucial part of the productivity picture. Most productivity advice focuses on all the possible ways we can get more done. But in focusing on this, we neglect to think about *the reasons we might be getting less done than what we're capable of.* We must identify what our productivity inhibitors are.

Let's say you have the goal of becoming as productive as possible at work. If this is your goal, you should focus on advice that falls into both categories. For starters, you should focus on strategies that let you work more intelligently and deliberately, and on what's important. This advice is fun to follow because of how immediate the results are. Strategies like planning out your week, keeping a to-do list, and saying no to unimportant work are all techniques that are helpful from the get-go. When you notice they work, you're more inclined to stick with them.

The second category of advice is tougher to master, far more neglected, yet just as critical if you care about your productivity level. In addition to focusing on ways you can get more done, you need to focus on all of the reasons you are getting less done than what you're capable of. This means paying attention to variables that limit your performance without your realizing it. Factors that put an unnecessary cap on how much you're able to accomplish include many ideas from this book, including:

- When you're burnt out because of the chronic stress you face, you become disengaged from what's right in front of you.
- Flying at an incredibly high stimulation height can lead you to procrastinate more and waste more time, because working on something essential means going from a high to a low height of stimulation.
- Constantly striving for more can lead you to become overly reliant on dopamine, which diminishes your capacity for presence.
- Spending too much time in front of screens can provide you with even more sources of hidden chronic stress.
- Anxious self-talk can cloud your judgment while distracting your mind from thinking about more important things, including planning projects, generating ideas, and reflecting on goals.
- Continually thinking about the opportunity cost of your time can prevent you from becoming immersed in the moment.

These are just a few factors that are tough to fix with a quick productivity hack. Left unchecked, they will lead us to become less calm, more anxious, and less productive.

## Anxiety and Productivity

With this in mind, let's calculate precisely how much less we accomplish while anxious.

For all of the reasons I've just mentioned, this has been a book about productivity as much as it has been about calm. The first type of productivity advice—which leads us to work smarter—is sexy and lets us get more done, especially at first. But by overinvesting in this category of advice and simultaneously neglecting to fix productivity deficits, we may become less productive than we'd like. This is especially true as time marches forward and we fail to focus on how much we've got left in the tank—mentally, emotionally, and even spiritually.

If you doubt the extent to which an anxious mental state can impair cognitive performance, you don't even need to take my word for it: you likely have many examples from your own life that illuminate this phenomenon. For example, think back to when you last had to give a speech in front of a group of people (if that sort of thing makes you nervous). You probably dreaded the event: public speaking is up there with death as one of our most common fears.

Recall what the state of your mind was like immediately before the talk. Could you focus easily, or did your mind barrage you with negative self-talk that hijacked your attention? Were you able to mentally process a lot at once—calmly carrying on conversations with whoever was around you—or were you busy fretting over what you were going to say? If, theoretically, before going onstage, someone had asked you to proofread something that required deep concentration, would you have been able to give it your full attention?

After your talk started, did you process it fully?

Do you remember what you said?

Maybe you're lucky, and you haven't given a speech in front of a large group of people, or perhaps you've spoken in front of enough groups that you've stepped back from these anxious thought patterns. If that's the case, think of the last time you flew on an airplane and hit a pocket of turbulence. If you were reading a book, did you have to re-read the same passage a few times? If you were listening to a podcast or watching a movie, did you need to rewind or mentally try to fill in the gaps of what you missed?

These are examples of anxiety compromising our cognitive performance. If anxiety is something you experience—even if that anxiety is subclinical—it probably limits your productivity in ways you don't yet realize. Your mind presumably (hopefully!) doesn't freeze up as much with everyday tasks as it does during something like a speech, airplane turbulence, or losing track of your kid in the department store. But these are good illustrations of an extreme, of how anxiety can compromise our attention and productivity without us realizing it.

Ironically, anxiety can make us less aware that our performance has plummeted because of how attentionally demanding it is in the first place.

## Anxiety and Attention

Our working memory capacity—which I like to call our "attentional space"—is a cognitive measure that supports us in pretty much everything we do. It's our immediate memory, and lets us hold information in our mind as we process and think about things in each moment. The more mental space we have to work with, the deeper we can think, the more we can process at one time, and the better we perform. A larger attentional space also provides us with a greater capacity to reflect on the events of our life. Our working memory aids our mental performance in almost every way by facilitating planning, comprehension, reasoning, problem-solving, and other critical functions.

Researchers have long understood that we become less productive as we become more anxious—this relationship has been studied for more than half a century. As one meta-analysis conducted by researcher Tim Moran summed up, "cognitive deficits are now widely recognized to be an important component of anxiety." It is now established that anxiety hinders our cognitive performance in numerous ways. For starters, it is reliably associated with "poorer performance on measures of reading comprehension and mathematical problem solving" and even "lower scores on standardized tests of intelligence and general aptitude [and] achievement."

The research suggests one common factor that these decreases in performance share: a diminished cognitive capacity. Anxiety is cognitively expensive. It leaves us with fewer resources to think. While studies contradict one another with just how much anxiety shrinks the size of our mental scratch pad, Moran has found that anxiety shrinks our attentional space by around 16.5 percent.

This sounds like a small number, but the effects of a slight decrease like this can be profound in practice—and not to mention this is just *one* way that anxiety affects our cognitive abilities. A shrunken attentional space means we process less in each moment. This gives us less mental freedom to think, piece together ideas, connect information, and make sense of the world in front of us. We may not be as unproductive as during airplane turbulence, but we can come very close.

Anxiety shrinks our capacity for accomplishment, consuming valuable attention while providing us with less ability to be present in our life.

Naturally, the more cognitively demanding your work is, the more that any amount of anxiety will hinder your performance. If your job involves repetitive actions that aren't as mentally taxing, as well as few relationships with other people, an anxious mind might not influence your performance that much.

But chances are the opposite is the case for you. A significant proportion of us now do knowledge work for a living—work that we do with our mind rather than with our hands.

A larger working memory capacity will help you immensely if you do knowledge work. Again, don't even take my word for it: think back to when your mind was far calmer and unburdened by an undercurrent of anxiety. The day after a long hike with friends, or refreshed after a disconnected vacation, how much more clearly were you able to think without anxious thoughts tugging at your focus? How deeply were you able to immerse yourself in what you were doing? With more attentional space, did you generate more ideas, feel more connected with those around you, and feel like you had more than enough cognitive resources at your disposal to do good work and live a good life?

A little mental capacity really does go a long way.

To gain a deeper understanding of just how much anxiety can hinder our mental capacity, I got in touch with Tim Moran to see how his thinking has evolved since he published the much-cited 2016 meta-analysis. The numbers haven't changed much. But in our discussions, he suggested an idea I found fascinating: beyond our working memory, anxiety seems to be associated with some factor that *limits our cognitive performance in general*. According to Moran, "the reason anxiety seems to be related to so many laboratory tasks and performance in real-life scenarios is that it is related to a higher general ability, like how much control we have over our attention—or even how well we're able to maintain our focus of attention in the face of competing information."

Put another way, anxiety doesn't just shrink our working memory. It effectively shrinks our mind. Regardless of what we do for a living, we must reclaim this lost mental capacity.

Moran's hunch isn't random—it has been informed by the thousands of studies he has pored over involving anxiety and cognitive performance. And new research supports his conclusions, suggesting that, in addition to occupying valuable attentional space, anxiety decreases how much *control* we have over our attention while also leading us to pay more attention to "threat-related stimuli."

We don't just have access to fewer mental resources during more anxious periods. While anxiety makes it significantly more challenging to focus, it also leads us to pay greater attention to novel threats—including sources of stress that are increasing our anxiety in the first place.

Our work and life benefit from all the brainpower we can possibly bring to them. Unfortunately for us, anxiety robs us of precious mental resources that we use to be productive and live a meaningful life.

In this exact way, investing in calm—and shrinking how anxious we feel, even if doing so takes time and energy—can save us more time than we think.

As a fun thought experiment, let's try to calculate exactly just how much we make back.

## Making Back Time

I should reiterate that not only are we all wired differently, but we also all live different lives and work vastly different jobs. On top of this, anxiety affects each of us differently—and, as a result, affects our performance by different amounts. This is especially true across different types of tasks. We use our attentional space to do three main things: manipulate and connect *knowledge*, process *visual* information, and process *auditory* information. Depending on how your anxiety manifests, your cognitive performance will be negatively affected in different ways.

If when you feel anxious you mostly find yourself paying attention to anxious *thoughts*, the general reasoning functionality of your working memory will be most negatively affected, and you may struggle to think logically as a result. If you find that you *visualize* anxious episodes from your past, the visuospatial sketch pad part of your attentional space may be most affected, and you may struggle with visual and spatial work. If you find that your negative *self-talk* runs rampant when you feel anxious, your attentional space's phonological (language) component may be most harmed, and you may not be able to communicate as effectively.

With all of these ideas in mind, let's try to ballpark how much time calm will save us. To illustrate how much time you can make back, let's make an incredibly conservative assumption that *the only way* that anxiety limits our performance is through a reduced working memory capacity. Let's also assume that the relationship between working memory and productivity is linear. In other words, for every percentage point decline in the size of our attentional space, our daily productivity declines by the same amount and takes that much longer as a result. Again, given how much we depend on this mental scratch pad, this is very likely a conservative measure.

When our attentional space size is 16.5 percent smaller, our work takes that much longer. This is a far more meaningful difference than it sounds: if we have eight hours of real, actual work to do, that workload now takes us *nine hours and nineteen minutes*.

If you've found yourself busier than you used to be as you've become more connected—yet upon a bit of reflection, your workload has stayed largely the same—anxiety could be why. (And given that workload is a critical contributor to burnout, this extra time may affect how engaged you are with your work, too.)

Anxiety doesn't have to be clinical for it to affect our performance. And it likely limits our productivity by a lot more than 16.5 percent because our working memory capacity is just one dimension of performance that anxiety affects.

Given that calm can lead us to so much—including to engagement, the process through which we actually make progress on our work—it can be considered a vital ingredient in productivity, especially during an anxious time. If you value productivity, the numbers are clear: you should absolutely invest in calm.

## Guilt at Work

As we invest in calm, guilt can arise for a couple of reasons.

The first place guilt can come from is the feeling that we're **not spending our time intentionally**. When we don't work with a high level of deliberateness, we can begin to worry about the opportunity cost of our time, as we doubt whether we're spending our time on the best possible thing.

This cause of guilt is easy enough to beat back, by investing in strategies that let you work more deliberately. Explore the first brand of productivity advice: the advice that lets you, as the cliché goes, work smarter and not harder. Define three daily priorities at work and at home, work with your manager to determine your most important tasks, and perhaps set an hourly awareness chime (many smart watches have this feature) to reflect more frequently on what you're working on. Maybe even pick up a productivity book if you want to get adventurous.

A second common reason guilt may arise is that **we're not acting in accordance with what we value**. Modern culture frowns upon inactivity. And when we accept the default values of our culture—that productivity, accomplishment, and constant progress matter above almost all else—guilt may arise as we invest in calm and become less busy. After all, we're not working hard during that time.

Most of us do value productivity to some degree. If that includes you, there are two main reasons why this second type of guilt is misplaced:

1. it's easy to gloss over just how much calm can help us achieve our goals, and
2. we're surprisingly bad at measuring how productive we are.

We touched on the first point a bit in the previous section. Assuming you have an average level of (subclinical) anxiety, eight hours of work takes you *at least* nine hours and nineteen minutes to do. This means if we spend eight hours at work every day, we frequently have to stay late, remain connected during the evenings, and work a few hours on weekends or when we're on vacation so as to not fall behind. This can result in a negative energy spiral that leads to the buildup of even more chronic stress—not to mention that you'll enjoy your time at work less. Dopamine begets dopamine, stimulation begets stimulation, and anxiety begets anxiety.

Of course, at work, the size of our attentional space is just one measure that matters. It's an important one, and explains why anxiety slows down our mind, leading us to remember less and process less at once—but there are other factors at play, too. At the same time that anxiety shrinks our attentional space, it also leads us to focus on less important things. This is especially the case for the more negative or threatening objects of attention we encounter. Embedded within anxiety is a phenomenon researchers call our "threat bias," which, as you might guess, leads us to pay more attention to anything in our environment that's threatening—including negative news stories and the catastrophizing thoughts in our head.

On top of this, anxiety makes us less productive in other ways. The mindset of more and superstimuli lead us to structure our habits around dopamine, which leads us to crave distraction. Anxiety makes us less engaged, while driving us to burnout. Superstimuli lead us to fly at a far higher altitude of stimulation than what is optimal for us to feel calm—and most of our productive tasks reside at a low stimulation height.

Given the myriad ways anxiety limits performance, it's not hard to see how an eight-hour day could take far longer than around nine and a half hours.

Using the numbers that we calculated in the last section—which become even more conservative once you account for all of these impacts of anxiety—the extent to which calm helps us break through our productivity barriers is obvious. It's even possible to calculate a "break-even point" of sorts, after which further investing in calm is not worthwhile. Let's assume that because of all of these additional impacts—less engagement, a diminished cognitive capacity, more stimulation, more self-talk, and less presence—your work takes you an additional twenty-five minutes a day, on top of the one hour and nineteen minutes you've already lost. The actual amount of time we lose is likely far more significant, but again, let's stay conservative so that nearly all of us earn back the calculated amount of time. Adding these twenty-five minutes to the amount of time we lose from our shrunken mental scratch pad, we now lose a total of *one hour and forty-four minutes* by working less effectively in an anxious state.

Framed another way, when we do knowledge work, we can spend nearly two hours a day investing in calm before we have to even *consider* whether we're becoming less productive.

It goes without saying that you won't need to spend this long investing in how calm you feel every day. Most of the tactics in this book—from confronting chronic stress to practicing presence to taming superstimuli—are designed to consume very little time, if any at all. Tactics like the dopamine fast might even save you time from the get-go. Nearly all tactics that require an investment of time fit in the previous chapter.

The moral of the anxiety story is a simple one: if you value productivity, you must invest in overcoming anxiety and finding calm. Investing in calm allows you to develop your capacity for productivity.

Better yet, you have no reason to feel guilty about investing this time, even if you're tempted to think about all of the more "productive" things you could be doing instead. If anything, the opposite is the case: you should feel guilty about *not* investing in calm because of how much more productive it will make you.

Here's an honest truth about investing in the strategies in this book: even once you understand, logically, how much more productive these tactics will make you, you may *still* feel guilty about spending time on them. At least I did, especially at first.

When this guilt arises, remind yourself how much more productive investing in calm is making you, without your realizing it. Then use this as a chance to reflect on the leftover guilt.

This is also a great opportunity to think about how you're measuring productivity in the first place.

## The Busyness Bias

It's difficult for us to measure how productive we are. Generally speaking, the more cognitively demanding your work is, the more difficult measuring your productivity becomes. When our work is mentally demanding and complex, what we produce with our time, attention, and energy is typically also just as complex.

Think back to the time when most people worked in factory production lines. This work was simple and repetitive—and measuring our productivity at the end of each day was straightforward. The more widgets we produced with a day's worth of our time, the more productive we were. On an eight-hour shift, we were twice as productive when we made eight widgets instead of four. There was a direct relationship between how much we produced, and our personal productivity.

With knowledge work, the quantity of our output no longer determines productivity.

If you were to write a 1,600-word report, you may feel four times as productive as when you write one that's 400. But what if that 400-word report effects more change at your company? What if it communicates more, while saving everyone time?

Here's another idea about guilt worth reflecting on. Which of these two reports do you *feel more productive* writing: the 1,600-word report or the 400-word one?

If you measure your work the traditional way, it's probably the one that either required more effort or took longer—not the one that actually made a difference or was the most useful.

These are the kinds of stories we tell ourselves about our productivity. On some level, we still equate output and energy expenditure with productivity—even when the connection between output, effort, and productivity has become severed with knowledge work.

Most of us don't give much thought to measuring how productive we are. But given how much of our lives we spend working—or just trying to do what we set out to do, without getting in our own way—this is a worthwhile question to think about: **How should we be measuring our productivity?**

Just as we also have ways of measuring whether a day went well, on some level, usually subconscious, we have ways of measuring how productive we are.

Because so many of us feel busy and stretched thin, we tend to look at more obvious cues that we were productive on a given day. We have the tendency to look at how hard we worked; how much raw effort we invested into getting stuff done. If we see signs that we've kept busy, our guilt vanishes. If we look back at a day of less activity, guilt can devour us whole—even if we accomplished more with a relaxed, deliberate day than with a day full of stimulating distraction.

Looking at how hard we work is not necessarily a bad thing—there are far worse measurements for productivity. That said, our impulse to measure our work this way tends to break down when measuring cognitive work. This is particularly true when our focus on energy expenditure prevents us from recharging, or leads us to work through a time when we should genuinely reflect on our projects and ideas. Blind busyness produces chronic stress, as we talked about in chapter 2.

It also leads us to fewer ideas. If you're a busy executive, taking a middle-of-the-day walk through the park might seem unproductive from the outside. But if doing so provides you with a billion-dollar idea that contributes more to your company than answering an entire *de-*

*cade's* worth of email, that's some of the best time you'll ever spend on anything. You'll *feel* less productive, but you're calm and energized and have identified a path to making a more substantive difference. Similarly, if you're a computer programmer, working fewer hours and taking more scatterfocus breaks to think about problems you're in the middle of may *save* you time overall. Or, if you're an administrative assistant, flying at a lower height of stimulation may also lead you to feel less productive—but you may also be able to move more projects forward as you cruise at a more comfortable altitude.

A calm mind is a deliberate mind, and a deliberate mind is a productive mind. If you feel the need to constantly "hustle," you're probably just overlooking significant opportunities to work more intelligently, including by investing in automating parts of your work and investing in calm.

**The trick to measuring productivity is to reflect on how much you accomplish.** Because our guilt from calm comes from the fact that, as we become less busy, we *feel* like we're making less progress, we must remind ourselves of the fruits that our efforts lead to. Because we tend to look at the wrong indicators that we had a productive day—how hard we worked, how many emails are left in our inbox, or how depleted we feel—it's essential that we provide our mind with concrete information about what results our time has led to. After all, it's entirely possible to work hard, reach inbox zero, and feel depleted without moving any of our important projects forward.

We need to track all we accomplish, especially as we become calmer, less busy, and more productive.*

---

* It should be said that in an office environment, the less busy you appear, the less productive you also look. Just as we're bad at measuring our own productivity, others are bad at measuring how productive we are. As French poet Pierre Reverdy put it, "There is no love. There are [only] proofs of love." The same can apply to productivity. In an ideal world, we're evaluated at work by how much we're able to accomplish. But in some

## Techniques for Guilt

Most of us want to become more productive and accomplished. But in practice, our mind looks to busyness and energy expenditure more often than it does to presence and deliberateness in assessing how productive we are. Luckily, there are ways of combating this. In doing so, we can remind ourselves of how much we accomplish, and experience less guilt while investing in calm.

Overcoming this guilt involves reflecting on what we accomplish so we can look at our days analytically, instead of reflexively and judgmentally. We have a mental bias, often called the "Zeigarnik effect" (named after psychologist Bluma Zeigarnik), that leads us to remember our unresolved commitments above everything we've gotten done. In the moment, the messy bedroom closet may weigh more heavily on our minds than all of our life's accomplishments put together.

Here are a few strategies that I've personally found helpful:

- **Keep a daily accomplishments list.** As each day progresses, write down all of the things you're able to get done. This is a tactic I've mentioned a couple of times already, and for a good reason: because of the Zeigarnik effect, we quickly forget about our daily wins. Review the items you've jotted down at the end of the day to remind yourself of your forgotten, completed tasks. As a general rule, you get more done than you think you do. This is an especially helpful tactic on days (or weeks) you feel like you're not moving anything forward.

cases, it could also be worthwhile to reflect on how productive you *come across*, in addition to how productive you are. Mind your proofs of productivity.

- **Maintain a longer-term accomplishments list, too.** In addition to the daily accomplishments list, I keep a file on my computer, dating back to 2012, with the accomplishments and milestones I've reached in my life and work—everything from anniversaries to work projects I've shipped to metrics I've hit with my business. Each year has about fifteen or twenty milestones or accomplishments nested underneath it, and it's fun to review the list at the beginning of every month to pick up momentum.

- **If you keep a to-do list or use a task manager, review what you've gotten done at the end of each day.** What do you do with your to-do list after the day is done? If you're like me before this project, you either crumpled up the list if it was analog or let completed tasks in your digital task manager evaporate into the digital ether. Be sure to look back at all your crossed-off items at the end of the day. Also, don't be afraid to add items to your list that you didn't plan on accomplishing. It's a great feeling to add something to the list just to cross it off (just because a victory was unintentional does not mean that it didn't happen).

- **Journal for a couple of minutes at the end of the day about how the day went.** At the end of the day, set a timer for a few minutes and recount how the day went; what you were able to accomplish, how deliberately you worked, what went well, and what you could improve on the next time around, including how you can become kinder to yourself as you work. Remember that this exercise is more of an opportunity to reflect on what went well than it is a chance to beat yourself up about what you want to change. This is a great tactic to do before you exit productivity mode.

These tactics might help you realize that you're more productive than you think you are. This is especially the case when you don't fill your days with busywork.

As you practice these tactics, be sure to reflect on how much you can accomplish before and after investing in calm.

Investing in calm helps you become less busy while making you more thoughtful, deliberate, and intentional. In these ways, calm can expand your capacity to get things done. To further crowd out the guilt of calm, reflect on the difference that calm makes in your work. Forming this kind of before-and-after mental picture can solidify the habits you develop.

As human beings, despite our two-hundred-thousand-year-old brain, we have countless skills: logic, reason, and creativity included. Unfortunately, measuring our productivity accurately is not one of them.

## Counterbalancing Productivity

I didn't set out on the journey that became this book for any other reason than to get past my own anxiety. I felt anxious, restless, and just generally uncomfortable in my own mind, and I knew something needed to give. Plus, if the very productivity advice I was investing in was driving me to burnout, it just wasn't working. Despite productivity being a significant interest of mine—who doesn't want to get more done of what they want?—if I couldn't find a way to avoid anxiety and burnout, I wasn't sure it was worth it.

Moving along the spectrum from anxiety toward calm, though, I stumbled upon a very different idea. By not investing in calm while investing in productivity, I was missing a critical part of the productivity picture, the ingredient that would make my work and life sustainable, meaningful, and enjoyable in the long run.

Anxiety doesn't just make us *less* productive. Calm makes us *more* productive. Think of the unflappable leader who makes difficult, thoughtful decisions under pressure; the journalist who can write a tight five-hundred-word breaking news story in thirty minutes; the doctor who can make their patients feel immediately at ease just by walking in the room. When it comes to productivity, calm matters.

Calm is an ingredient that helps us accomplish more of what we want. In an anxious environment, we become productive when we approach our work with a calm deliberateness, when we stay present, focused, and resilient against distraction. As we settle down into a lower stimulation level, focus becomes effortless. And as we invest in presence, we lead ourselves out of burnout and become more engaged in the process. We enjoy our work and life more, while accomplishing more of what matters.

Hooked on dopamine and stress, we feel productive. But as we talked about earlier, that's just a mirage of productivity. It's not hard to see how the very values that our culture holds dear—such as accumulation, consumption, and the general acquisition of *more*—can prove antithetical to calm, particularly in the long run.

The first brand of productivity advice—which lets us work smarter—is important. But in an anxious world full of chronic stress and dopaminergic distraction, calm easily matters just as much.

There is a certain tranquil quality to devoting our entire capacity for presence to one thing. It's a feeling of sinking in, of becoming the very thing you're engaging with. Instead of hammering a nail, the hammer becomes a part of you, an extension of your hand. Instead of writing a letter with a ballpoint pen, the pen becomes a vessel through which you channel your thoughts, the synapses in your brain firing in a way that converts your ideas into precise micro-movements in the pen's rollerball tip.

In an odd way, at its best, productivity can be borderline *meditative*, a set of practices that let us become wholly immersed in whatever we want to be doing in the moment. If we're able to become fully, deeply present with the things we intend to accomplish—directing our full time, attention, and energy toward those activities—we never really have to worry about productivity.

Calm improves our productivity enough to make it worth striving for on its own—even if you are not an anxious person. The presence that calm cultivates is easily worth the time investment—especially given that presence is a key to productivity.

But at the end of the day, productivity is just one benefit. Calm truly is a beautiful end in and of itself. The calmer we become, the more at ease we feel, both with our own lives and the world around us. We can exhale an easy sigh, let our shoulders down, and just be with our life. We sink deeper into each moment, while either savoring or making progress with what's in front of us.

As you lower your stimulation height and focus more easily, you'll feel great about striking more items off your to-do list. But the feeling of being free from empty dopamine hits that don't make you happy? That's the real payoff, especially in the long run. You'll enjoy your life more, not bounding between dopaminergic distractions.

In this same way, if you've ever been burnt out—or come close to being so—you'll know how raw, unfair, and devastating the state can feel, regardless of how luxurious your situation looks from the outside.

Developing an ability to be present with your work, which leads you away from exhaustion, cynicism, and feeling like you're not making a difference . . . this is perhaps the biggest prize of all.

Calm doesn't just lead you to make a more significant difference. It also gives you the capacity to realize that you already do.

## CHAPTER NINE

## Where Calm Lives

Close to two years after I experienced the onstage panic attack, the sun would break through for me.

I had tried quite a few things to find calm during that time: from ideas that made the cut into this book to tactics that didn't work nearly as well. That included both therapy and CBD oil, two tactics people wondered about when I mentioned that I was trying to cultivate calm in my life.

I found therapy to be fun, and a great way to discover why my mind is conditioned the way it is. But it didn't lead me to as much calm as more pragmatic strategies like the stimulation fast, or dealing with the preventable items on my stress inventory. (Of course, your mileage will probably vary: if you're a curious person like me, I highly recommend seeing a therapist if doing so is within your budget. You're bound to learn a few exciting and interesting things about your mind. And, if you think your anxiety may be clinical—if it sticks around regardless of what tactics you try—therapy is probably worthwhile.)

Unfortunately, trying CBD oil had similarly underwhelming effects for me. CBD can be derived from two main sources: the hemp plant, and the cannabis plant, which has a shadier reputation. As luck would have it for this experiment, cannabis was legalized for recreational purposes in Canada around when I embarked on my journey to calm.

Simplified, there are two main components of cannabis: THC and CBD. THC is the psychoactive component that intoxicates you, which can make you feel some combination of euphoria, hunger, paranoia, relaxation, and sleepiness, along with a warped perception of time—all depending on the strain of plant you consume and your own wiring. CBD is the nonpsychoactive component of the plant, which has purported benefits for afflictions like pain, anxiety, and arthritis.

While there is not much peer-reviewed, scientific evidence that CBD helps with conditions like these, I was too curious after legalization to not give in to the hype and give it a shot. Doing my absolute best not to look like a square, I put on the mental equivalent of a fake mustache and walked downtown to a local cannabis shop to see what they recommended for anxiety. I arrived home thirty minutes later with three little tincture bottles of oil. I placed half a dropper's worth of one of them under my tongue to see what would happen—and after looking out for changes, felt nothing, to my surprise. The next day, I doubled up. Still nothing. The following day, I downed a couple more dropperfuls. I still didn't feel much. This time, with the supersized dose, my mind felt quieter and a bit spaced out, but no less anxious than before. After trying a few other brands, I found I didn't benefit much from the stuff. (On a caffeine-equivalency scale, the strength of the effect felt equal to a cup or two's worth of green tea—though as you know by now, I keep my caffeine tolerance low.)

Of all the things I experimented with in my journey to find calm, I felt the most let down by CBD, which I truly did not expect. Unfortunately, the research supports my anecdotal account. As one meta-analysis put it, "There is a lack of evidence that cannabinoids [CBD] improve depressive disorders and symptoms, anxiety disorders, attention-deficit hyperactivity disorder, Tic/Tourette syndrome, post-traumatic stress disorder, or psychosis"—all conditions that some purport the chemical compound helps with. There is a bit of evidence that THC, the active component, "leads to a small improvement in symptoms of anxiety amongst those with other medical conditions." While more research should be conducted (and is currently being conducted), CBD oil may not be worth your hard-earned money. But as always, your mileage may vary. Some people swear by it—and even if the most you ever feel is a calming placebo, it may be worthwhile.

This is a bummer—especially when we're all looking for a quick fix when it comes to anxiety, the one strategy, pill, or dropperful of something we can take that makes the anxiety go away. In the immediate term, the best we can do is dampen anxiety, to take our mind off the fact that it's there. It takes effort to go deeper, to unearth the root causes of why we're unsettled in the first place; the factors that can tilt our mind toward the anxious side of the calm spectrum. Often, we have to make structural changes to our habits and lives.

Luckily, making these more difficult changes is almost always worthwhile. By dealing with the root causes of why we're anxious, we live a life more faithful to who we are and what we value, while feeling more comfortable in our own skin. The effects of these improvements can be simple, like that we no longer struggle to get off Instagram—or better yet, that we crave less time on chronically stressful social media updates in the first place. They can also prove even more profound. For example, we might no longer feel exhausted, cynical, and unproductive after switching to a job that contains a far more manageable level of chronic stress.

Regardless of the changes you've made thus far, I hope you find that calm is and has been worth the investment. This is true even for the calm strategies that require an investment of time, like cooking up delicious, healthy dinners, finding a form of movement you deeply enjoy, or spending time with good friends.

## Trying Things Out

Throughout this book, I've offered up a lot of strategies for finding steadiness in an overanxious world. Whether you're looking to overcome feelings of anxiety, want to find greater meaning in the events of your life, or just want to sink more comfortably into each moment, the ideas contained herein should help. The same is true if you intend to use these ideas to cultivate more free time, satisfaction, or presence. You can also use the ideas in the book to unlock greater productivity and creativity; calm is a sturdy foundation for both work and life, and presence is what productivity is all about.

As we wrap things up, one of the last things I want to encourage you to do is **try out as many strategies in this book as possible**. Not all of the strategies will work for you. But by throwing a bunch of (evidence-based) tactics at the proverbial wall, you can see what naturally sticks and what you enjoy the most. If I found one thing to be true in my journey to calm, it's that calm is *personal*. We're all wired differently, lead different lives, and have different habits, jobs, constraints, and values. Because of this, I encourage you to take the advice that works for you and leave the rest. (This is a helpful strategy to use not just for this book, but for the other pragmatic nonfiction books you read, too.)

There are countless ideas you can try. Try moving more, in nature if you can. Practice meditation, a way of developing a more vibrant presence with everything you do. Create a personalized savor list, and enjoy one thing on it every day. Inventory the stress in your life to identify low-hanging sources you can tame. Define productivity hours so you can strike a daily balance between striving and savoring. Undertake a monthlong stimulation fast to make focus effortless and settle your mind. Choose a few "currencies" in your life that you personally want to strive for more of—like happiness, presence, and time with other people—instead of the defaults like money and status. Invest in habits of calm in the analog world that lead your body to release serotonin, oxytocin, and endorphins, along with a healthy and more reasonable amount of dopamine. Notice and question the guilt that arises as you invest in calm. See a therapist if you want to dig deeper into your mind.

Pick one or two things from this list. And while you're at it, make a plan to try more things out after you've tried the first couple. Set aside a few hours each week to go analog only, or try some new analog hobbies, like taking an improv class, cooking, learning an instrument, or knitting. As an experiment, subscribe to a physical newspaper, while swearing off digital news for a while. Reconnect with play, or treat yourself to a one-hour massage each time you ship a big work project. Make a plan to cut back on liquor, or try resetting your caffeine tolerance. Maybe even write a letter or two to a loved one with a fancy fountain pen.

As I know you'll find, calm is a worthwhile pursuit in and of itself. Trying out as many tactics as you can—whether small or large, straightforward or structural—is what lets you find what strategies actually fit with who you are, and the life you live. Doing this will also make calm sustainable over time.

## Finding Enough

It is sometimes said that all we need to feel happy is right in front of us, but this doesn't feel true when the mindset of more gets in our way.

The mindset of more tells the opposite story: that happiness lies ever so slightly beyond what we have, what we've accomplished, and who we currently are. As soon as we make a bit more money, become a bit more productive, or become a bit fitter, *then* we'll be comfortable, and then (and only then) do we believe we will have the time and attention to enjoy the fruits of what we've accomplished.

In practice, we really just push the goalposts a little beyond our reach—and never stop doing so.

Here's a simple truth: regardless of how much you have, comfort, calm, and happiness will come from savoring the things that are already in your life—not from trying to get what you do not have. Adopting this mindset takes practice and patience, and happens over time as you invest in habits of calm. But as I found, it's well worth the effort.

Up until the calm project, I personally felt as though I never had enough. This was true even for areas of my life that were objectively going well. Looking at how many books my author colleagues were selling, I felt like I was continually falling behind, never doing quite well enough to deserve happiness. (The truth, painfully obvious to everyone but me, was that I'm lucky to be in this line of work in the first place.) Making a bonus through work, and saving that money, I would remind myself how far I still had to go to attain some level of financial freedom. The truth, of course, was I was lucky to even have the extra income to save.

By default, we look for satisfaction in the exact wrong place: in what we don't have, rather than what we do. Luckily for us, a calm mind converts these feelings of inadequacy into gratitude. When we learn to become present with who and what are in front of us, we'll always feel as though we have enough.

While investing in calm shifted my priorities around a tad, how I felt *inside* changed far more. I enjoyed my days more deeply, because I became more present in them. And I had the energy, stamina, and motivation for what came my way.

As we've covered, the idea of *more* is a mirage. Not only can we always accumulate more of the various currencies in our life, but the things we desire more of also often conflict with one another. The modern world will tell us that more will bring us happiness. But the very last place we should be taking happiness advice from is the modern world. The modern world is not happy. Instead, we need to look inside.

The more I invested in calm, the more present and happy I became with my life. Investing in tactics like enjoying the items on my savor list, spending more time in the analog world, and doing additional stimulation fasts whenever distractions crept back in, I was able to find comfort in most moments of the day. I would be lying if I said that I felt completely calm all of the time; there were still periods when I felt anxious or encountered events that led me to feel threatened and anxious.

But over time, anxious spells like these would become more the exception than the norm, an occasional feeling as ephemeral as a short-lived gust of wind in the park. The fruits of calm proved profound.

I hope you'll find what I did, that investing in calm leads you to become even more grateful for all you have in your life—and that it does so while letting you reflect on which currencies are worth striving for more of. Either way, whether you seek more time, attention, energy, relationships, depth, freedom, recognition, or even money, keep in mind that true abundance is savoring what you already have.

## Deeper Connections

Another exciting benefit you may experience when you cultivate calm is a greater awareness of what's happening in your body and mind.

Nearly every moment of the day, our body and mind are trying to tell us something, like that we're low on energy (and should recharge), or that we're getting fatigued or already exhausted. Other times our body and mind are reminding us that we're already full of food, have had more than enough caffeine, or that we need to confront how we're feeling instead of watching one more episode of some show. Or they're reminding us to be grateful, to slow down enough to enjoy things, or to savor every moment we have with someone, because there will only be so much time left with them. The more awareness we have, the more intentionally we can act. Calm means there's less happening in our mind in each moment, which gives us the space we need to reflect and notice.

On top of this awareness, another benefit of reaching more profound levels of calm is that you also become more intentional.

Intention is when you decide what to do ahead of doing it—and it's possible to observe your mind forming an intention just by giving it a little more space. As a simple experiment, the next time you feel like listening to music, instead of choosing your go-to playlist, wait a few seconds until your mind comes up with the perfect song that you want to listen to. That's what it feels like for an intention to form.

In making us more likely to notice our intentions, calm can make us feel more accomplished—further combating burnout. When we choose what to do ahead of doing it, we feel more efficacious in our actions. By becoming more intentional about what we spend our time on, and deciding what to do ahead of time, we feel our actions have a purpose, even when we don't have total control over our work or life. Our efforts don't change, but our mindset and stories do: we feel as though we're *choosing* to take on things that are difficult and stressful—they're no longer things that happen *to* us. Regardless of our level of control, calm gives intentions room to form and allows us to notice and then act on them.

By becoming more aware and intentional through calm, we're also able to further solidify the place calm has in our lives. We may have the attentional space to observe that Instagram is making us depressed, and have the wherewithal to delete the app for a few months to see if we feel any different. In an argument, we're able to find calmer footing and say the *second* thing that comes to mind rather than speaking impulsively. When we're about to eat past the point of fullness (and regret), our mind becomes still enough to notice that we're full so we don't climb down an emotional-eating escape hatch.

Through stepping back—not just in general, but in each moment—we gain perspective.

Anxiety clouds awareness and intention. Luckily, by investing in calm, we're able to reflect and become more deliberate. The dust in our minds settles, and we see things more clearly.

## After Calm

Back when the sun broke through in my own story, the world was becoming dimmer. In March 2020, just as I was reconnecting after my first dopamine fast, pandemic case numbers began accelerating around the globe.

To me, the series of events at the start of the COVID-19 pandemic are hazy in hindsight, one big ball of a timeline that has only gotten more stuck together with time. The dopamine fast experiment was a refreshing break from this worry: instead of constantly reloading news websites, the paper offered my morning briefing before I went on with my day.

That was until I couldn't.

Near the end of the experiment, the pandemic had been labeled a global health emergency by the World Health Organization, and travel to the US from China was restricted (which felt bonkers at the time). I reconnected with the world as lockdowns, quarantines, and social distancing were becoming part of our newfound pandemic lexicon, when we were all trying to make sense of how to react to this new, uncertain world. Back online after my experiment, I found it was tough to look away. And for a while, I didn't. For March and April of 2020, it was as if my stimulation fast hadn't happened. I was glued to one screen or another, checking which events were canceled, how case numbers were changing, and what newfangled restrictions were being put into place.

I had done a lot of work up to this point to introduce habits of calm into my life, while balancing my mind so calm had space to thrive. While the start of a global pandemic meant I temporarily stopped following some of this advice, the work I had done allowed me to quickly revert to the habits I had cultivated in the months prior. It took my noticing that I was feeling anxious again to trigger a return to these practices, but given the "unprecedented" state of the world, I call that a win.

I'm not sure I would have even noticed the increase in anxiety if it weren't for the space calm had created in the first place. The structural changes I made during my experiments became a shield to protect my mind against a suddenly very anxious world.

Alongside the structural changes I had made to my work and life, I thankfully also had a host of calm habits I could fall back on. The more anxious the world became, the more I doubled down. Instead of checking digital news throughout the day, I subscribed to a second physical newspaper to get a more balanced blend of local and international news. Instead of anxiety-scrolling around social media, I exercised and meditated. I ratcheted down my caffeine consumption. I got lost in paperback books, found things to savor each day, and coordinated plenty of video calls with friends and family, until that became a tiring proposition for everyone. I also made a concerted effort to find more analog hobbies—getting into photography, working out, and going on hikes with my wife.

On top of all this, I made sure to take the time to apply the brakes and enjoy some slow moments. If anxiety is rushed and hurried, calm is patient and forgiving. While I wasn't always successful, I tried to carry this spirit of calm with me throughout the day.

Two years after March 2020, calm is even more present in my life. If anything, I've discovered that finding calm is a skill we can get better at over time.

As I write these words, the winter's snow is melting and turning to slush, washing away the sand and salt that piles on top of decaying autumn leaves. Inside and away from the elements, the situation is less subdued. Deadlines are piling up (this book's manuscript is due in two weeks, for example), the news is still worrisome, and on a surface level, much of my work is the same as at the start of this journey into calm. The rhythms of work and life carry on: snow falls and melts, periods of busyness come and go, and each new season of life offers varying amounts of stress, novelty, and opportunity.

Beneath these rhythms of daily life, however, the difference could not be more profound.

If today's Chris and the Chris before this journey were to stand on opposite sides of a mountain, we'd likely describe an entirely different landmark, even though we're essentially looking at the same thing from a different angle. This is akin to the difference before and after calm.

Life gets busy, and we're often pushed to our mental limits. Investing in strategies for calm may change our situation, but how we *relate* to our situation will change even more. We live much the same life, but see it from a calmer perspective.

After exploring and investing in the strategies I've shared in this book, I'm still busy, but for the most part I'm no longer anxious. I've become less emotionally reactive as the circumstances around me have changed. When I do feel anxiety on any given day, it's blunted and more fleeting—usually a response to some acutely stressful thing. I have developed habits that reliably lead me away from anxiety and toward calm. And each day, I feel as though I have the mental fortitude to do a good job of what I plan to do.

During particularly stressful periods, calm has afforded me the ability to step back, introduce space between myself and the situation, and find firm footing during otherwise anxious times. This hasn't always been easy. Hell, finding this space isn't even always *possible*. Luckily, though, cultivating calm is a skill we can all get better at. We can all learn to see the same mountain in a different light.

I began this book with the story of my onstage anxiety attack. The writer inside me wishes for some crescendo of a story to balance out this book, some exciting climax to counterweight the dramatic event that kicked off my journey to calm in the first place. But after living through the journey that led to this book, here's the honest truth: I really don't want one.

Calm is not a crescendo; it is a winding down, a returning to our true nature. It's the state of our mind that lies beneath the layers of activity in our life.

Calm is not all that exciting, *and that is precisely the point*. As we cultivate calm, we replenish our mental capacity to handle and enjoy excitement that comes our way. Instead of our mind being overstimulated by default, it's calm, and above all else, *ready*. With calm as our default state of mind, we can rise to the height of what happens.

Calm habits give us the stamina to handle stressful new situations. With less chronic stress, we become engaged and can pragmatically find solutions to problems, while also being mentally present for the best parts of our day. And with greater focus comes more productivity, which lets us carve out more time for life—and for habits of calm—in the first place.

Throughout these pages, I've done my best to provide ideas, tactics, and strategies you can use on your own journey to calm—ones I'm confident will help you find more space, presence, and productivity. But here's one more thought experiment before you go: If the path to calm were an *actual* path, what might it look like?

For starters, the trail would most definitely run right through nature, rather than a city street. You might walk it at a brisk pace to elevate your heart rate—and maybe you would have eaten a delicious, nutritious meal beforehand so you have energy for the steps ahead. You'd probably also be soaking in the sun, and the path would wind through the analog world—you wouldn't be walking in some video game. You'd probably also be strolling in the company of others.

Along the way, a leisurely presence will come over you. And hopefully, you'll find yourself immersed, appreciating each step.

The walk will take time. But given you'll find yourself with energy, stamina, and focus, those minutes and hours spent will not be lost. In all likelihood, you'll have made them back and then some.

Calm is a wellspring at the heart of what makes life enjoyable. From it springs productivity, presence, insight, intention, awareness, comfort, good humor, acceptance, creativity, and gratitude.

It is also our natural state of being, hidden beneath the layers of busyness in our life. Calm underscores everything we do, everything we think, and everything we believe we are. It is our life when we eliminate each layer of unnecessary activity: mental busyness, the busyness of doing too much, the busyness of working long hours, engaging with superstimuli, accumulating more than what we need, or trying to be more productive than we need to be.

Purposeful busyness is what makes life worth living—a life devoid of purpose is one devoid of meaning. But because of how much more enjoyable life becomes with calm by our side, I hope you'll agree that it's worth the pursuit.

To remain comfortable, present, and productive in a sea of chaos; while the world whips itself into a frenzy; when there are so many concerns, worries, and cares tugging at our limited time . . . that is a gift that we can give ourselves.

At its core and at its best, calm can be considered the foundation for a good life.

I hope this book helps you find it.

# Acknowledgments

Every single day, I feel grateful to work alongside incredible, generous, smart people.

Thank you first to my wife, Ardyn (who has all three of those characteristics in spades). Ardyn is my favorite person in the world to bounce ideas around with, and my books would not be what they are without her input, support, and feedback. Ardyn, I hope you'll always be my first reader. I love you.

On the publishing front, a giant thank-you to my editors at Penguin Group (US), Random House Canada, and Pan Macmillan UK. Rick, Craig, and Mike, it is a true privilege to get to work with you. Thank you, sincerely, for all of your support and guidance—and for the opportunity to share these ideas with others.

I also feel grateful to work with everyone *else* at Penguin, Random House Canada, and Macmillan. At Penguin, a special thank-you to Ben Petrone, Camille LeBlanc, Sabila Khan, Lynn Buckley, Lydia Hirt, and Brian Tart. At Random House Canada, thank you to Sue Kuruvilla and

Chalista Andadari. At Pan Macmillan, thank you to Lucy Hale, Natasha Tulett, Josie Turner, and Stuart Wilson.

Thank you also to my superstar agent, Lucinda Halpern. Lucinda, I can't believe we've already done three books together. I can't wait to see what the future brings. It's a gift to get to do these projects with you—whether they were intended or not!

This project would also not be possible without the help of individuals who provided support and advice along the way. Thank you to Amanda Perriccioli Leroux for her invaluable support, especially when I'm traveling or taking one of my many work sabbaticals or think breaks. Thank you to Victoria Klassen and Hilary Duff, who were kind enough to provide edits for and feedback on the manuscript. Thank you to Anna Nativ for her genius design support and to Ryan Wilfong for his help with my new website. Thank you to Anne Bogel, Katherine Chen, Camille Noe Pagán, and Laura Vanderkam for their invaluable advice and guidance. And thank you to David, Ernie, Mike S., Mike V., and Nick for the conversation, friendship, and food for thought.

Thank you also to the countless researchers referenced in the Notes section of this book. I stand on your shoulders—I hope that I have done your work justice and it has the chance to help even more people because of this book.

It really does take a village.

Thank you to my family, especially my parents, Colleen and Glen; to my sister, Emily; to Jamie, Anabel, and Elijah; and to Steve, Helene, Morgan, Deb, Alfonso, and Sarah.

Finally, thank you to you. I really mean it. Every day I feel like the luckiest person in the world because I get to write about these ideas that I find fascinating. I get to keep doing this because people like you buy my art, and for that I'm incredibly grateful. I hope you have found the ideas in this book worthy of your time and attention—and that your mind is calmer because of the ideas in these pages.

# Notes

## CHAPTER TWO: STRIVING FOR ACCOMPLISHMENT

17 **In her book *The Writing Life*:** Dillard, Annie. *The Writing Life*. New York: Harper-Perennial, 1990.

17 **Thanks to economic progress:** Noell, Edd. *Economic Growth: Unleashing the Potential of Human Flourishing*. Washington, DC: AEI Press, 2013.

18 **Twenty years ago, 29 percent:** Rosling, Hans, Ola Rosling, and Anna Rosling Rönnlund. *Factfulness: Ten Reasons We're Wrong about the World—and Why Things Are Better Than You Think*. London: Hodder & Stoughton, 2019.

18 **"The main factor that affects how people live":** Rosling, Rosling, and Rönnlund. *Factfulness*.

22 **Most of us know what calm:** *Cambridge Dictionary*, s.v. "Calm." Accessed March 1, 2022. https://dictionary.cambridge.org/us/dictionary/english/calm; and *Merriam-Webster*, s.v. "Calm." Accessed March 1, 2022. https://www.merriam-webster.com/dictionary/calm.

22 **After many hours of scouring:** de Lemos, Jane, Martin Tweeddale, and Dean Chittock. "Measuring Quality of Sedation in Adult Mechanically Ventilated Critically Ill Patients." *Journal of Clinical Epidemiology* 53, no. 9 (September 2000): 908–19. https://www.doi.org/10.1016/s0895-4356(00)00208-0.

23 **Importantly, while anxiousness is:** Posner, Jonathan, James A. Russell, and Bradley S. Peterson. "The Circumplex Model of Affect: An Integrative Approach to Affective Neuroscience, Cognitive Development, and Psychopathology." *Development and Psychopathology* 17, no. 3 (September 2005): 715–34. https://www.doi.org/10.1017/S0954579405050340.

23 **Research has confirmed that calm:** Siddaway, Andy P., Peter J. Taylor, and Alex M. Wood. "Reconceptualizing Anxiety as a Continuum That Ranges from High

Calmness to High Anxiety: The Joint Importance of Reducing Distress and Increasing Well-Being." *Journal of Personality and Social Psychology* 114, no. 2 (February 2018): e1–11. https://www.doi.org/10.1037/pspp0000128.

23 **In this state, we are:** Nock, Matthew K., Michelle M. Wedig, Elizabeth B. Holmberg, and Jill M. Hooley. "The Emotion Reactivity Scale: Development, Evaluation, and Relation to Self-Injurious Thoughts and Behaviors." *Behavior Therapy* 39, no. 2 (June 2008): 107–16. https://www.doi.org/10.1016/j.beth.2007.05.005.

31 **We human beings were nothing:** Dunn, Rob. "What Are You So Scared of? Saber-Toothed Cats, Snakes, and Carnivorous Kangaroos." *Slate.* October 15, 2012. https://slate.com/technology/2012/10/evolution-of-anxiety-humans-were-prey-for-predators-such-as-hyenas-snakes-sharks-kangaroos.html.

31 **As psychologist Kelly McGonigal:** McGonigal, Kelly. *The Upside of Stress: Why Stress Is Good for You, and How to Get Good at It.* New York: Avery, 2015.

32 **as Facebook whistleblower Frances Haugen:** Paul, Kari. "Facebook Whistleblower Hearing: Frances Haugen Testifies in Washington—as It Happened." *The Guardian.* October 5, 2021. https://www.theguardian.com/technology/live/2021/oct/05/facebook-hearing-whistleblower-frances-haugen-testifies-us-senate-latest-news.

33 **One study found that participants:** Holman, E. Alison, Dana Rose Garfin, and Roxane Cohen Silver. "Media's Role in Broadcasting Acute Stress following the Boston Marathon Bombings." *Proceedings of the National Academy of Sciences of the United States of America* 111, no. 1 (January 7, 2014): 93–98. https://www.doi.org/10.1073/pnas.1316265110.

33 **Another study found that watching:** Thompson, Rebecca R., et al. "Media Exposure to Mass Violence Events Can Fuel a Cycle of Distress." *Science Advances* 5, no. 4 (April 17, 2019). https://www.doi.org/10.1126/sciadv.aav3502.

## CHAPTER THREE: THE BURNOUT EQUATION

45 **As the World Health Organization defines it:** "Burn-Out an 'Occupational Phenomenon': International Classification of Diseases." World Health Organization. May 28, 2019. https://www.who.int/news/item/28-05-2019-burn-out-an-occupational-phenomenon-international-classification-of-diseases.

46 **Giving a three-hour lecture:** Segerstrom, Suzanne C., and Gregory E. Miller. "Psychological Stress and the Human Immune System: A Meta-analytic Study of 30 Years of Inquiry." *Psychological Bulletin* 130, no. 4 (July 2004): 601–30. https://www.doi.org/10.1037/0033-2909.130.4.601.

46 **Researchers describe that it's as though:** Michel, Alexandra. "Burnout and the

Brain." *Observer* 29, no. 2 (February 2016). https://www.psychologicalscience.org/observer/burnout-and-the-brain.

46 **Studies suggest that those diagnosed:** Oosterholt, Bart G., et al. "Burnout and Cortisol: Evidence for a Lower Cortisol Awakening Response in both Clinical and Non-clinical Burnout." *Journal of Psychosomatic Research* 78, no. 5 (May 2015): 445–51. https://www.doi.org/10.1016/j.jpsychores.2014.11.003.

47 **cortisol levels in the morning:** Bush, Bradley, and Tori Hudson. "The Role of Cortisol in Sleep." *Natural Medicine Journal* 2, no. 6 (2010). https://www.naturalmedicinejournal.com/journal/2010-06/role-cortisol-sleep.

49 **Cynicism is a feeling:** Leiter, Michael P., and Christina Maslach. "Latent Burnout Profiles: A New Approach to Understanding the Burnout Experience." *Burnout Research* 3, no. 4 (December 2016): 89–100. https://www.doi.org/10.1016/j.burn.2016.09.001.

50 **One study found that 59 percent:** Maske, Ulrike E., et al. "Prevalence and Comorbidity of Self-Reported Diagnosis of Burnout Syndrome in the General Population." *Psychiatrische Praxis* 43, no. 1 (2016): 18–24. https://doi.org/10.1055/s-0034-1387201; and Koutsimani, Panagiota, Anthony Montgomery, and Katerina Georganta. "The Relationship between Burnout, Depression, and Anxiety: A Systematic Review and Meta-Analysis." *Frontiers in Psychology* 10 (March 13, 2019): 284. https://www.doi.org/10.3389/fpsyg.2019.00284.

50 **In one study, 58 percent:** Maske et al. "Prevalence and Comorbidity of Self-Reported Diagnosis of Burnout Syndrome in the General Population."

50 **While the exact relationship among:** Bakusic, Jelena, et al. "Stress, Burnout and Depression: A Systematic Review on DNA Methylation Mechanisms." *Journal of Psychosomatic Research* 92 (January 2017): 34–44. https://www.doi.org/10.1016/j.jpsychores.2016.11.005.

50 **identify whether you have the resources:** Leiter and Maslach. "Latent Burnout Profiles."

52 **"So much of how we":** Maslach, Christina, interview by Chris Bailey, December 14, 2020.

52 **As Maslach has written:** Maslach, Christina. "Finding Solutions to the Problem of Burnout." *Consulting Psychology Journal* 69, no. 2 (June 2017): 143–52. https://www.doi.org/10.1037/cpb0000090.

53 **"Burnout is viewed":** Maslach, interview.

53 **This means that in an:** Eschner, Kat. "The Story of the Real Canary in the Coal Mine." *Smithsonian Magazine*, December 30, 2016. https://www.smithsonianmag.com/smart-news/story-real-canary-coal-mine-180961570.

53 **At one such workplace:** Maslach, interview.

54 **Another is one that she:** "Depression: What Is Burnout?" *Institute for Quality and*

*Efficiency in Health Care.* June 18, 2020. https://www.ncbi.nlm.nih.gov/books/NBK279286.

54 **While the experiment was disastrous:** Zimbardo, Philip. *The Lucifer Effect: Understanding How Good People Turn Evil.* New York: Random House, 2008.

54 **As Maslach would later put it:** Zimbardo, Philip G., Christina Maslach, and Craig Haney. "Reflections on the Stanford Prison Experiment: Genesis, Transformations, Consequences." In *Obedience to Authority: Current Perspectives on the Milgram Paradigm*, ed. Thomas Blass, 207–52. New York: Psychology Press, 1999.

55 **as found in one meta-analysis:** Salvagioni, Denise Albieri Jodas, et al. "Physical, Psychological and Occupational Consequences of Job Burnout: A Systematic Review of Prospective Studies." *PLOS One* 12, no. 10 (October 4, 2017): e0185781. https://www.doi.org/10.1371/journal.pone.0185781.

59 **six areas of our work act as Petri dishes:** Leiter, Michael P., and Christina Maslach. "Six Areas of Worklife: A Model of the Organizational Context of Burnout." *Journal of Health and Human Services Administration* 21, no. 4 (Spring 1999): 472–89. https://www.jstor.org/stable/25780925.

59 **The first factor of the six:** Leiter and Maslach. "Six Areas of Worklife."

60 **Ideally, we have a workload:** Csikszentmihalyi, Mihaly. *Flow: The Psychology of Optimal Experience.* New York: Harper Perennial, 1991.

60 **The second source of burnout:** Leiter and Maslach. "Six Areas of Worklife."

60 **Research shows that the more:** Maslach, Christina, and Cristina G. Banks. "Psychological Connections with Work." In *The Routledge Companion to Wellbeing at Work*, ed. Cary L. Cooper and Michael P. Leiter, 37–54. New York: Routledge, 2017.

60 **One common source:** Maslach. "Finding Solutions to the Problem of Burnout."

60 **Third, insufficient reward:** Leiter and Maslach. "Six Areas of Worklife."

60 **One study found that, if you're a manager:** Achor, Shawn. *Big Potential: How Transforming the Pursuit of Success Raises Our Achievement, Happiness, and Well-Being.* New York: Currency, 2018.

61 **The fourth burnout factor:** Leiter and Maslach. "Six Areas of Worklife."

61 **We derive an immense amount:** Maslach. "Finding Solutions to the Problem of Burnout"; and Maslach and Banks. "Psychological Connections with Work."

61 **Fairness is the fifth factor:** Leiter and Maslach. "Six Areas of Worklife."

61 **Maslach defines fairness as:** Maslach and Banks. "Psychological Connections with Work."

61 **The sixth and final burnout:** Leiter and Maslach. "Six Areas of Worklife."

61 **Research suggests that our values:** Maslach. "Finding Solutions to the Problem of Burnout."

62 **Pay particular attention to the workload:** Leiter and Maslach. "Six Areas of Worklife."

## CHAPTER FOUR: THE MINDSET OF MORE

72 **our happiness begins to level off:** Kahneman, Daniel, and Angus Deaton. "High Income Improves Evaluation of Life but Not Emotional Well-Being." *Proceedings of the National Academy of Sciences of the United States of America* 107, no. 38 (September 21, 2010): 16489–93. https://www.doi.org/10.1073/pnas.1011492107.

72 **This is well illustrated by a study:** Robin, Vicki, and Joe Dominguez. *Your Money or Your Life: 9 Steps to Transforming Your Relationship with Money and Achieving Financial Independence: Revised and Updated for the 21st Century.* 2nd ed. New York: Penguin, 2008.

73 **Savoring is our mind's ability:** Bryant, Fred B., and Joseph Veroff. *Savoring: A New Model of Positive Experience.* Mahwah, NJ: Lawrence Erlbaum Associates, 2007.

73 **One study found that merely being *exposed*:** Quoidbach, Jordi, et al. "Money Giveth, Money Taketh Away: The Dual Effect of Wealth on Happiness." *Psychological Science* 21, no. 6 (June 2010): 759–63. https://www.doi.org/10.1177/0956797610371963.

74 **As social psychologist Leon Festinger:** Festinger, Leon. "A Theory of Social Comparison Processes." *Human Relations; Studies towards the Integration of the Social Sciences* 7, no. 2 (May 1954): 117–40. https://www.doi.org/10.1177/001872675400700202.

75 **As author Seth Godin has written:** Godin, Seth. *The Practice: Shipping Creative Work.* New York: Portfolio, 2020.

75 **To paraphrase Maya Angelou:** Tunstall, Elizabeth Dori. "How Maya Angelou Made Me Feel." *The Conversation,* May 29, 2014. http://theconversation.com/how-maya-angelou-made-me-feel-27328.

76 **Dopamine is a neurochemical:** Hamilton, Jon. "Human Brains Have Evolved Unique 'Feel-Good' Circuits." Stanford University, November 30, 2017. https://neuroscience.stanford.edu/news/human-brains-have-evolved-unique-feel-good-circuits.

76 **But research suggests that dopamine:** Moccia, Lorenzo, et al. "The Experience of Pleasure: A Perspective between Neuroscience and Psychoanalysis." *Frontiers in Human Neuroscience* 12 (September 4, 2018): 359. https://www.doi.org/10.3389/fnhum.2018.00359.

76 **Research shows that our brain:** Moccia et al. "The Experience of Pleasure."

76 **As Daniel Lieberman, the coauthor:** Lieberman, Daniel Z., and Michael E. Long. *The Molecule of More: How a Single Chemical in Your Brain Drives Love, Sex, and*

*Creativity—and Will Determine the Fate of the Human Race.* Dallas: BenBella Books, 2019.

77 **Ambition is another fascinating:** Judge, Timothy A., and John D. Kammeyer-Mueller. "On the Value of Aiming High: The Causes and Consequences of Ambition." *Journal of Applied Psychology* 97, no. 4 (July 2012): 758–75. https://www.doi.org/10.1037/a0028084.

78 **As defined by another team:** Krekels, Goedele, and Mario Pandelaere. "Dispositional Greed." *Personality and Individual Differences* 74 (February 2015): 225–30. https://www.doi.org/10.1016/j.paid.2014.10.036.

82 **Neuroscientists like Lieberman:** Lieberman and Long. *The Molecule of More.*

83 **The main neurochemicals that:** Breuning, Loretta Graziano. *Habits of a Happy Brain: Retrain Your Brain to Boost Your Serotonin, Dopamine, Oxytocin, & Endorphin Levels.* Avon, MA: Adams Media, 2016.

83 **Much as a dopamine-centered:** Lieberman and Long. *The Molecule of More.*

84 **Yet another fascinating discovery:** Maslach, Christina, and Michael P. Leiter. "Understanding the Burnout Experience: Recent Research and Its Implications for Psychiatry." *World Psychiatry* 15, no. 2 (June 2016): 103–11. https://www.doi.org/10.1002/wps.20311.

89 **"greater savoring capability":** Bryant, Fred B., and Joseph Veroff. *Savoring: A New Model of Positive Experience.* London: Psychology Press, 2017.

90 **As the researchers who conducted:** Quoidbach et al. "Money Giveth, Money Taketh Away."

90 **Driven by dopamine, we rarely:** Joel, Billy. "Vienna." Accessed July 1, 2020. https://billyjoel.com/song/vienna-2.

92 **On average, we experience around:** Gable, Shelly L., and Jonathan Haidt. "What (and Why) Is Positive Psychology?" *Review of General Psychology* 9, no. 2 (June 2005): 103–10. https://www.doi.org/10.1037/1089-2680.9.2.103.

93 **In his research, Bryant:** Bryant and Veroff. *Savoring.*

93 **High levels of savoring:** Hou, Wai Kai, et.al. "Psychological Detachment and Savoring in Adaptation to Cancer Caregiving." *Psycho-Oncology* 25, no. 7 (July 2016): 839–47. https://www.doi.org/10.1002/pon.4019.

93 **One study found that the act:** Hurley, Daniel B., and Paul Kwon. "Results of a Study to Increase Savoring the Moment: Differential Impact on Positive and Negative Outcomes." *Journal of Happiness Studies* 13, no. 4 (August 2012): 579–88. https://www.doi.org/10.1007/s10902-011-9280-8; and Smith, Jennifer L., and Fred B. Bryant. "The Benefits of Savoring Life: Savoring as a Moderator of the Relationship between Health and Life Satisfaction in Older Adults." *International Journal of Aging and Human Development* 84, no. 1 (December 2016): 3–23. https://www.doi.org/10.1177/0091415016669146.

94 **Savoring is the art of enjoying:** Fritz, Charlotte, and Morgan R. Taylor. "Taking in the Good: How to Facilitate Savoring in Work Organizations." *Business Horizons* 65, no. 2 (March–April 2022): 139–48. https://www.doi.org/10.1016/j.bushor.2021.02.035.

94 **flow is different because:** Bryant and Veroff. *Savoring.*

94 **Savoring is also different:** Fritz and Taylor. "Taking in the Good."

94 **"Just because you've obtained something":** Bryant and Veroff. *Savoring.*

95 **Bryant's research indicates:** Bryant and Veroff. *Savoring.*

95 **One theory for why:** Chun, HaeEun Helen, Kristin Diehl, and Deborah J. MacInnis. "Savoring an Upcoming Experience Affects Ongoing and Remembered Consumption Enjoyment." *Journal of Marketing* 81, no. 3 (May 2017): 96–110. https://www.doi.org/10.1509/jm.15.0267.

## CHAPTER FIVE: HEIGHTS OF STIMULATION

99 **Over five hundred *hours*:** "YouTube: Hours of Video Uploaded Every Minute 2019." Statista. May 2019. https://www.statista.com/statistics/259477/hours-of-video-uploaded-to-youtube-every-minute.

99 **YouTube is the second-largest search engine globally:** "The Top 500 Sites on the Web." Alexa. Accessed July 29, 2021. https://www.alexa.com/topsites.

99 **Localized versions of YouTube:** "YouTube for Press." YouTube. Accessed July 29, 2021. https://www.youtube.com/intl/en-GB/about/press.

100 **YouTube can also be considered:** "Most Popular Social Networks Worldwide as of April 2021, Ranked by Number of Active Users." Statista. April 2021. https://www.statista.com/statistics/272014/global-social-networks-ranked-by-number-of-users.

104 **It has earned this proportion:** "How Long Will Google's Magic Last?" *The Economist*, December 2, 2010. https://www.economist.com/business/2010/12/02/how-long-will-googles-magic-last.

104 **Facebook made *97 percent*:** "Facebook's Annual Revenue from 2009 to 2020, by Segment." Statista. January 2021. Accessed March 4, 2022. https://www.statista.com/statistics/267031/facebooks-annual-revenue-by-segment/.

104 **Together, the two companies:** Perrin, Nicole. "Facebook-Google Duopoly Won't Crack This Year." eMarketer. Insider Intelligence. November 4, 2019. https://www.emarketer.com/content/facebook-google-duopoly-won-t-crack-this-year.

104 **To assemble your list of interests:** Bryan, Chloe. "Instagram Lets You See What It Thinks You Like, and the Results Are Bizarre." Mashable. June 5, 2019. https://mashable.com/article/instagram-ads-twitter-game.

108 **The internet is chock-full:** Brooks, Mike. "The Seductive Pull of Screens That You Might Not Know About." *Psychology Today.* October 17, 2018. https://www .psychologytoday.com/ca/blog/tech-happy-life/201810/the-seductive-pull -screens-you-might-not-know-about.

110 **Research shows that three factors influence:** Lieberman, Dan, interview by Chris Bailey, January 8, 2021.

110 **There are numerous diseases:** Caligiore, Daniele, et al. "Dysfunctions of the Basal Ganglia-Cerebellar-Thalamo-Cortical System Produce Motor Tics in Tourette Syndrome." *PLOS Computational Biology* 13, no. 3 (March 30, 2017). https:// www.doi.org/10.1371/journal.pcbi.1005395; Davis, K. L., et al. "Dopamine in Schizophrenia: A Review and Reconceptualization." *American Journal of Psychiatry* 148, no. 11 (November 1991): 1474–86. https://www.doi.org/10.1176/ajp .148.11.1474; Gold, Mark S., et al. "Low Dopamine Function in Attention Deficit/ Hyperactivity Disorder: Should Genotyping Signify Early Diagnosis in Children?" *Postgraduate Medicine* 126, no. 1 (2014): 153–77. https://www.doi.org/10.3810/pgm .2014.01.2735; Ashok, A. H., et al. "The Dopamine Hypothesis of Bipolar Affective Disorder: The State of the Art and Implications for Treatment." *Molecular Psychiatry* 22, no. 5 (May 2017): 666–79. https://www.doi.org/10.1038/mp.2017.16; Walton, E., et al. "Exploration of Shared Genetic Architecture between Subcortical Brain Volumes and Anorexia Nervosa." *Molecular Neurobiology* 56, no. 7 (July 2019): 5146–56. https://www.doi.org/10.1007/s12035-018-1439-4; Xu, Tian, et al. "Ultrasonic Stimulation of the Brain to Enhance the Release of Dopamine—A Potential Novel Treatment for Parkinson's Disease." "4th Meeting of the Asia-Oceania Sonochemical Society (AOSS 2019)." Ed. Jun-Jie Zhu and Xiaoge Wu. Special issue, *Ultrasonics Sonochemistry* 63 (May 2020): 104955. https://www.doi .org/10.1016/j.ultsonch.2019.104955; and Tost, Heike, Tajvar Alam, and Andreas Meyer-Lindenberg. "Dopamine and Psychosis: Theory, Pathomechanisms and Intermediate Phenotypes." *Neuroscience and Biobehavioral Reviews* 34, no. 5 (April 2010): 689–700. https://www.doi.org/10.1016/j.neubiorev.2009.06.005.

111 **70 percent of men are regular users of porn:** Wilson, Gary. *Your Brain on Porn: Internet Pornography and the Emerging Science of Addiction.* Margate, UK: Commonwealth, 2015.

112 **"build [the] pursuit of novelty":** Wilson. *Your Brain on Porn.*

112 **"after consumption of pornography":** Zillmann, Dolf, and Jennings Bryant. "Pornography's Impact on Sexual Satisfaction." *Journal of Applied Social Psychology* 18, no. 5 (April 1988): 438–53. https://www.doi.org/10.1111/j.1559-1816.1988 .tb00027.x

112 **In many cases, porn:** Wilson. *Your Brain on Porn.*

113 **"situations in which rewards are unexpectedly obtained":** Steinberg, Eliza-

beth E., et al. "A Causal Link between Prediction Errors, Dopamine Neurons and Learning." *Nature Neuroscience* 16, no. 7 (July 2013): 966–73. https://www.doi.org /10.1038/nn.3413.

114  **this is called the "mere exposure effect":** Robinson, Brent M., and Lorin J. Elias. "Novel Stimuli Are Negative Stimuli: Evidence That Negative Affect Is Reduced in the Mere Exposure Effect." *Perceptual and Motor Skills* 100, no. 2 (April 2005): 365–72. https://www.doi.org/10.2466/pms.100.2.365-372.

114  **a stimulus is positive, neutral, or negative:** Robinson and Elias. "Novel Stimuli Are Negative Stimuli."

115  **This may not be by chance:** Fiorillo, Christopher D., Philippe N. Tobler, and Wolfram Schultz. "Discrete Coding of Reward Probability and Uncertainty by Dopamine Neurons." *Science* 299, no. 5614 (2003): 1898–1902. https://www.doi.org /10.1126/science.1077349.

115  **James Clear, the author of *Atomic Habits*:** Clear, James. *Atomic Habits: An Easy & Proven Way to Build Good Habits & Break Bad Ones.* New York: Avery, 2018.

122  **Dopamine is addictive:** Moccia, Lorenzo, Marianna Mazza, Marco Di Nicola, and Luigi Janiri. "The Experience of Pleasure: A Perspective between Neuroscience and Psychoanalysis." *Frontiers in Human Neuroscience* 12 (September 2018): 359. https://doi.org/10.3389/fnhum.2018.00359.

124  **Only staying active:** García, Héctor, and Francesc Miralles. *Ikigai: The Japanese Secret to a Long and Happy Life.* New York: Penguin Books, 2017.

## CHAPTER SIX: STIMULATION FASTING

135  **serotonin makes us feel important:** Breuning, Loretta Graziano. *Habits of a Happy Brain: Retrain Your Brain to Boost Your Serotonin, Dopamine, Oxytocin, & Endorphin Levels.* Avon, MA: Adams Media, 2016.

136  **Serotonin also protects us:** Emmons, Henry. *The Chemistry of Calm: A Powerful, Drug-Free Plan to Quiet Your Fears and Overcome Your Anxiety.* New York: Touchstone, 2011.

137  **almost nothing makes us more present:** Killingsworth, Matthew A., and Daniel T. Gilbert. "A Wandering Mind Is an Unhappy Mind." *Science* 330, no. 6006 (November 12, 2010): 932. https://www.doi.org/10.1126/science.1192439.

138  **I also meditated more:** Lieberman, Daniel Z., and Michael E. Long. *The Molecule of More: How a Single Chemical in Your Brain Drives Love, Sex, and Creativity—and Will Determine the Fate of the Human Race.* Dallas: BenBella Books, 2019.

142  **One study found that negative:** Soroka, Stuart, and Stephen McAdams. "News, Politics, and Negativity." *Political Communication* 32, no. 1 (2015): 1–22. https://www .doi.org/10.1080/10584609.2014.881942.

142 **Another study that analyzed weekly:** Erisen, Elif. *"Negativity in Democratic Politics.* By Stuart N. Soroka. (Cambridge University Press, 2014)" (review). *Journal of Politics* 77, no. 2 (April 2015): e9–10. https://www.doi.org/10.1086/680144.

143 **Research suggests that superstimuli:** Mrug, Sylvie, Anjana Madan, Edwin W. Cook III, and Rex A. Wright. "Emotional and Physiological Desensitization to Real-Life and Movie Violence." *Journal of Youth and Adolescence* 44, no. 5 (May 2015): 1092–108. https://doi.org/10.1007/s10964-014-0202-z.

144 **In one study, participants who:** Smith, Jennifer L., and Fred B. Bryant. "Savoring and Well-Being: Mapping the Cognitive-Emotional Terrain of the Happy Mind." In *The Happy Mind: Cognitive Contributions to Well-Being*, 139–56. Cham, Switzerland: Springer International, 2017.

144 **In another study, participants who abstained:** Smith and Bryant. "Savoring and Well-Being."

144 **wise, legendary investor Warren Buffett:** Kane, Colleen. "Homes of Billionaires: Warren Buffett." CNBC, July 26, 2012. https://www.cnbc.com/2012/07/26/Homes -of-Billionaires:-Warren-Buffett.html; Gates, Bill, and Melinda Gates. "Warren Buf-fett's Best Investment." GatesNotes (blog), February 14, 2017. https://www.gates notes.com/2017-Annual-Letter.

152 **We can learn, for example:** Blakemore, Sarah-Jayne. "The Social Brain in Ado-lescence." *Nature Reviews Neuroscience* 9, no. 4 (April 2008): 267–77. https://www .doi.org/10.1038/nrn2353.

152 **The best evidence suggests:** Robson, David. "A Brief History of the Brain." *New Scientist*, September 21, 2011. https://www.newscientist.com/article/mg21128311 -800-a-brief-history-of-the-brain.

153 **Exercise used to be:** Lieberman, Daniel E. *The Story of the Human Body: Evolution, Health, and Disease.* New York: Vintage Books, 2014.

## CHAPTER SEVEN: CHOOSING ANALOG

155 **average American spent over ten hours per day:** "COVID-19: Screen Time Spikes to over 13 Hours per Day according to Eyesafe Nielsen Estimates." Eyesafe, March 28, 2020. https://eyesafe.com/covid-19-screen-time-spike-to-over-13-hours -per-day.

155 **More recent data:** "COVID-19: Screen Time Spikes to over 13 Hours per Day Ac-cording to Eyesafe Nielsen Estimates." Eyesafe.

162 **Research suggests that the less:** Bailey, Chris. *Hyperfocus: How to Be More Productive in a World of Distraction.* New York: Viking, 2018.

167 **Historically, we evolved to walk:** Lieberman, Daniel E. *The Story of the Human Body: Evolution, Health, and Disease.* New York: Vintage Books, 2014.

167 **Now we get around:** Althoff, Tim, et al. "Large-Scale Physical Activity Data Re-

veal Worldwide Activity Inequality." *Nature* 547, no. 7663 (July 20, 2017): 336–39. https://www.doi.org/10.1038/nature23018.

167 **One study found that the number's:** Tudor-Locke, Catrine, and David R. Bassett Jr. "How Many Steps/Day Are Enough?: Preliminary Pedometer Indices for Public Health." *Sports Medicine* 34, no. 1 (January 2004): 1–8. https://www.doi.org /10.2165/00007256-200434010-00001.

168 **Here's a rule worth living:** Laskowski, Edward R. "How Much Should the Average Adult Exercise Every Day?" Mayo Clinic, April 27, 2019. https://www.mayo clinic.org/healthy-lifestyle/fitness/expert-answers/exercise/faq-20057916.

168 **She's a firm believer that:** McGonigal, Kelly. *The Joy of Movement: How Exercise Helps Us Find Happiness, Hope, Connection, and Courage.* New York: Avery, 2021.

169 **As McGonigal said to me:** Bailey, Chris. "Want to Become Happier? Get Moving!" *A Life of Productivity*, June 16, 2020. https://alifeofproductivity.com/want-to -become-happier-get-moving.

170 **"When you move in synchronicity":** Bailey. "Want to Become Happier?"

170 **Studies show that we experience:** Bailey. "Want to Become Happier?"

170 **McGonigal's research suggests that outdoor exercise:** Bailey. "Want to Become Happier?"

171 **loneliness is as damaging to our overall health:** Birak, Christine, and Marcy Cuttler. "Why Loneliness Can Be as Unhealthy as Smoking 15 Cigarettes a Day." CBC News, August 17, 2017. https://www.cbc.ca/news/health/loneliness-public -health-psychologist-1.4249637.

171 **that the strength of our social circles:** Ducharme, Jamie. "Why Spending Time with Friends Is One of the Best Things You Can Do for Your Health." *Time*, June 25, 2019. https://time.com/5609508/social-support-health-benefits.

171 **What they found was staggering:** Holt-Lunstad, Julianne, et al. "Loneliness and Social Isolation as Risk Factors for Mortality: A Meta-analytic Review." *Perspectives on Psychological Science* 10, no. 2 (March 2015): 227–37. https://www.doi.org /10.1177/1745691614568352.

174 **Stanford professor Jamil Zaki wrote:** Zaki, Jamil. "'Self-Care' Isn't the Fix for Late-Pandemic Malaise." *The Atlantic*, October 21, 2021. https://www.theatlantic .com/ideas/archive/2021/10/other-care-self-care/620441.

177 **One study found that meditation:** Harte, Jane L., Georg H. Eifert, and Roger Smith. "The Effects of Running and Meditation on Beta-Endorphin, Corticotropin-Releasing Hormone and Cortisol in Plasma, and on Mood." *Biological Psychology* 40, no. 3 (June 1995): 251–65. https://www.doi.org/10.1016/0301-0511(95)05118-t.

179 **This activity will allow:** Howland, Robert H. "Vagus Nerve Stimulation." *Current Behavioral Neuroscience Reports* 1, no. 2 (June 2014): 64–73. https://www.doi .org/10.1007/s40473-014-0010-5; Baenninger, Ronald. "On Yawning and Its Functions." *Psychonomic Bulletin & Review* 4, no. 2 (June 1997): 198–207. https://www

.doi.org/10.3758/BF03209394; Wile, Alfred L., Brandon K. Doan, Michael D. Brothers, and Michael F. Zupan, "Effects of Sports Vision Training on Visual Skill Performance: 2189 Board #160 May 30 9:00 AM -10:30 AM." *Medicine & Science in Sports & Exercise* 40, no. 5 (May 2008): S399. https://www.doi.org/10.1249/01.mss .0000322701.18207.3b.

181 **A lack of sleep is a:** Vgontzas, Alexandros N., et al. "Chronic Insomnia Is Associated with Nyctohemeral Activation of the Hypothalamic-Pituitary-Adrenal Axis: Clinical Implications." *Journal of Clinical Endocrinology & Metabolism* 86, no. 8 (August 2001): 3787–94. https://www.doi.org/10.1210/jcem.86.8.7778.

181 **Caffeine stimulates the release:** Garrett, Bridgette E., and Roland R. Griffiths. "The Role of Dopamine in the Behavioral Effects of Caffeine in Animals and Humans." *Pharmacology, Biochemistry, and Behavior* 57, no. 3 (July 1997): 533–41. https://www.doi.org/10.1016/s0091-3057(96)00435-2.

182 **Caffeine has been shown:** Lovallo, William R., et al. "Caffeine Stimulation of Cortisol Secretion across the Waking Hours in Relation to Caffeine Intake Levels." *Psychosomatic Medicine* 67, no. 5 (September 2005): 734–39. https://www.doi .org/10.1097/01.psy.0000181270.20036.06; Lane, J. D., et al. "Caffeine Effects on Cardiovascular and Neuroendocrine Responses to Acute Psychosocial Stress and Their Relationship to Level of Habitual Caffeine Consumption." *Psychosomatic Medicine* 52, no. 3 (May 1990): 320–36. https://www.doi.org/10.1097/00006842 -199005000-00006.

183 **Caffeine consumption has long been:** Hughes, R.N. "Drugs Which Induce Anxiety: Caffeine." *New Zealand Journal of Psychology* 25, no.1 (June 1996): 36–42.

184 **There is caffeine lurking in:** "Caffeine Chart." Center for Science in the Public Interest. Accessed July 28, 2021. https://cspinet.org/eating-healthy/ingredients-of -concern/caffeine-chart.

185 **L-theanine is an:** Mehta, Foram. "What You Should Know about L-Theanine." *Healthline*, January 20, 2021. https://www.healthline.com/health/l-theanine.

186 **around 54.9 percent of Americans over eighteen have had a drink:** "Alcohol Facts and Statistics." National Institute on Alcohol Abuse and Alcoholism. Accessed March 4, 2022. https://www.niaaa.nih.gov/publications/brochures-and-fact -sheets/alcohol-facts-and-statistics.

186 **Binge drinking is defined:** "Alcohol Facts and Statistics."

186 **Surprisingly, alcohol consumption:** "Alcohol Facts and Statistics."

186 **As George F. Koob:** Stiehl, Christina. "Hangover Anxiety: Why You Get 'Hangxiety' after a Night of Drinking." *Self*, January 1, 2021. https://www.self.com/story /hangover-anxiety.

187 **research shows that alcohol affects the production:** Banerjee, Niladri. "Neurotransmitters in Alcoholism: A Review of Neurobiological and Genetic Studies."

*Indian Journal of Human Genetics* 20, no. 1 (2014): 20–31. https://www.doi.org/10.4103/0971-6866.132750.

187 **First, alcohol leads our brain to produce:** Banerjee. "Neurotransmitters in Alcoholism."

187 **Unfortunately, serotonin production is suppressed:** Banerjee. "Neurotransmitters in Alcoholism."

187 **Alcohol also affects GABA:** Banerjee. "Neurotransmitters in Alcoholism."

189 **With higher blood sugar:** Franklin, Carl, Jason Fung, and Megan Ramos. "Stress and Weight Gain," December 13, 2017. The Obesity Code Podcast. 48:05. https://podcasts.apple.com/us/podcast/stress-and-weight-gain/id1578520037?i=1000530185283.

189 **Anxiety, depression, and insomnia:** Timonen, M., et al. "Depressive Symptoms and Insulin Resistance in Young Adult Males: Results from the Northern Finland 1966 Birth Cohort." *Molecular Psychiatry* 11, no. 10 (October 2006): 929–33. https://www.doi.org/10.1038/sj.mp.4001838.

189 **During stressful periods, 40 percent:** Dallman, Mary F. "Stress-Induced Obesity and the Emotional Nervous System." *Trends in Endocrinology & Metabolism* 21, no. 3 (March 2010): 159–65. https://www.doi.org/10.1016/j.tem.2009.10.004.

189 **Those who have a bit of extra:** Kershaw, Erin E., and Jeffrey S. Flier. "Adipose Tissue as an Endocrine Organ." *Journal of Clinical Endocrinology & Metabolism* 89, no. 6 (June 2004): 2548–56. https://www.doi.org/10.1210/jc.2004-0395.

189 **During periods of high stress, we have:** Dallman. "Stress-Induced Obesity."

189 **And when we feel sad:** Berridge, Kent C., and Terry E. Robinson. "What Is the Role of Dopamine in Reward: Hedonic Impact, Reward Learning, or Incentive Salience?" *Brain Research Reviews* 28, no. 3 (December 1998): 309–69. https://www.doi.org/10.1016/s0165-0173(98)00019-8.

190 **According to Henry Emmons:** Emmons, Henry. *The Chemistry of Calm: A Powerful, Drug-Free Plan to Quiet Your Fears and Overcome Your Anxiety.* New York: Touchstone, 2011.

## CHAPTER EIGHT: CALM AND PRODUCTIVE

199 **You probably dreaded the event:** Dwyer, Karen Kangas, and Marlina M. Davidson. "Is Public Speaking Really More Feared Than Death?" *Communication Research Reports* 29, no. 2 (2012): 99–107. https://www.doi.org/10.1080/08824096.2012.667772.

201 **Our working memory aids:** Cowan, Nelson. "Working Memory Underpins Cognitive Development, Learning, and Education." *Educational Psychology Review* 26, no. 2 (June 2014): 197–223. https://www.doi.org/10.1007/s10648-013-9246-y.

201 **As one meta-analysis conducted:** Moran, Tim P. "Anxiety and Working Memory Capacity: A Meta-analysis and Narrative Review." *Psychological Bulletin* 142, no. 8 (August 2016): 831–64. https://www.doi.org/10.1037/bul0000051.

201 **The research suggests one common factor:** Moran. "Anxiety and Working Memory Capacity."

201 **Moran has found that anxiety shrinks:** This is a measure that I adapted from Moran's paper, "Anxiety and Working Memory Capacity: A Meta-analysis and Narrative Review." In the analysis, Moran measures the extent to which anxiety shrinks working memory capacity, but his result is measured in standard deviations. To convert this figure into a simple correlation measure, I converted the standard deviation measure to Cohen's d (based on Hedges and Olkin, 1985) to estimate the correlation associated with the original effect size (using Rosenthal, 1984). This outputted the final result: -16.47 percent. I contacted Moran to confirm that I interpreted his results correctly, and he got the same thing. It is difficult to communicate just how much conflicting research there is about how anxiety affects our working memory capacity—this makes his paper even more relevant and vital. It's the best resource that I have found that analyzes the extent to which anxiety affects working memory capacity.

202 **"the reason anxiety seems to be related":** Moran, Tim, interview by Chris Bailey, June 10, 2021.

203 **And new research supports his conclusions:** Eysenck, Michael W., et al. "Anxiety and Cognitive Performance: Attentional Control Theory." *Emotion* 7, no. 2 (May 2007): 336–53. https://www.doi.org/10.1037/1528-3542.7.2.336.

204 **We use our attentional space:** Chai, Wen Jia, Aini Ismafairus Abd Hamid, and Jafri Malin Abdullah. "Working Memory from the Psychological and Neurosciences Perspectives: A Review." *Frontiers in Psychology* 9 (March 2018): 401. https://www.doi.org/10.3389/fpsyg.2018.00401; and Lukasik, Karolina M., et al. "The Relationship of Anxiety and Stress with Working Memory Performance in a Large Non-depressed Sample." *Frontiers in Psychology* 10 (January 2019): 4. https://www.doi.org/10.3389/fpsyg.2019.00004.

207 **a phenomenon researchers call our "threat bias":** Azarian, Bobby. "How Anxiety Warps Your Perception." BBC, September 29, 2016. https://www.bbc.com/future/article/20160928-how-anxiety-warps-your-perception.

212 **We have a mental bias:** Baddeley, A. D. "A Zeigarnik-like Effect in the Recall of Anagram Solutions." *Quarterly Journal of Experimental Psychology* 15, no. 1 (March 1963): 63–64. https://www.doi.org/10.1080/17470216308416553.

## CHAPTER NINE: WHERE CALM LIVES

220 **a lack of evidence that cannabinoids:** Black, Nicola, et al. "Cannabinoids for the Treatment of Mental Disorders and Symptoms of Mental Disorders: A Sys-

tematic Review and Meta-analysis." *The Lancet: Psychiatry* 6, no. 12 (December 2019): 995–1010. https://www.doi.org/10.1016/S2215-0366(19)30401-8.

221 **There is a bit of evidence that THC:** Black et al. "Cannabinoids for the Treatment of Mental Disorders."

227 **Near the end of the experiment:** "Coronavirus Declared Global Health Emergency by WHO." BBC News, January 31, 2020. https://www.bbc.com/news/world-51318246.

# Index

Italicized page numbers indicate material in tables or illustrations.